TRYALS

&

TRYBULATIONS

A'DRIANA LAFAYE

Copyright © 2019 A'Driana LaFaye

ISBN: 978-0-578-55716-8

Year of First Printing: 2019

Self-Published: A'Driana LaFaye

P.O. BOX 1929 Lawrenceville, GA 30046

Cover Model: Sherrell Turner

Graphic Artist: Rebecca (Golden Signature Art)

Book Cover: Fiverr - NookShawn

Formatted by: Saleh Joy

Edited by: All Write Editing, Inc.

DEDICATION

This book is dedicated to anyone who thought their dreams would never come true. For anyone who's only stumbling block is yourself. I am proof that you can achieve whatever you put your mind to.

I can do all things through Christ which strengthens me.   Philippians   4:13

Contents

Acknowledgments

There are so many people that kept me motivated and encouraged during this process. First and foremost, I want to thank God for giving me the vision and the content to write. I want to thank my husband, for his love and support as well as both my sons. I want to thank all my family that has pushed me, given me referrals, and encouraged me along the way. I want to thank my god mom for constantly staying on me to ensure my voice is heard in the form of this book series. And finally, I want to thank my close friends that would never allow me to settle with being my stumbling block.

1.

DANITA

Danita walked out onto her country-style porch and thought about how beautiful the weather was. The air was crisp, there were leaves everywhere, and it was a comfortable sixty degrees. It was a perfect day for a gathering.

Danita had been cooking all morning and was tired. Normally, she would have Thanksgiving dinner at her home, supply the turkey and the ham and have her family bring the remainder of the food. However, this year, she decided she wanted to prepare the whole dinner herself. She made a smoked turkey, honey-glazed ham, fried catfish, mustard greens mixed with turnip greens and smoked turkey tails, squash casserole, macaroni and cheese, dressing with gravy, chitterlings, broccoli and rice casserole, creamed corn, green beans, candied yams, and Hawaiian Sweet Rolls. She made desserts the night before, peach cobbler, sweet potato and pumpkin pie, banana pudding, and red velvet cake with cream cheese and pecans.

Danita sat on the swing that her late husband hand built for her and absorbed the scenery. Her estate was in Peachtree City, Georgia, about forty-five minutes outside of Atlanta. It sat on five acres of flat land that seemed to stretch to the horizon. The home itself was four-sided stucco with three levels, eight bedrooms, and six and a half bathrooms. She often thought about if she needed all that space, especially now that it was just her in the home. While she anxiously awaited her family's arrival; it seemed as though they were always late; she was a little on edge about a letter she received the day before. She could not help but ponder over what to do about it. The letter was from Jeremy, her first boyfriend and her oldest son's birth father. Danita pulled the letter out of her pocket and read over it again.

Jeremy Greene

545 Godby Rd

College Park GA 30349

404-323-5986

Hey, Danita its Jeremy. I know I am probably the last person you want to hear from. I have been out of jail for a while now. I turned my life around. I contemplated for a long time on whether or not I should send you this letter, but I realized it would not be right if I did not try to make contact. I would like to see you and my son. Yes, I know about our child. My mom told me about him before she died. I understand why you kept that from me. I was a different person then. I know he is older now, but I would still like to meet him. There are so many things that I want to say to you but are better said in person. I hope that you will respond to my letter so we can talk. I really am looking forward to meeting him and seeing you again.

Jeremy

Tears ran down Danita's face as she folded the letter back up and put it into her pocket. He was right; he is the last person she would have ever expected to contact her. "How did he even find out where I lived," she wondered. She had not thought about him in years. This letter created so many confusing thoughts. She had never told her son about his real father. Danita started to think about their first encounter.

She met Jeremy her senior year in high school. She had been moping around for weeks because the date she planned to go to the prom with backed out when he found out that sex was not on the agenda. Prom was three weeks away, and she was dateless. She was standing at her locker talking to a friend when a young tall Caucasian guy with beautiful blue eyes and blonde hair approached her and asked if she had a date for the prom.

Danita was stunned. First of all, she did not know this person and had never seen him before. Secondly, he was gorgeous. He had beautiful eyes and lips. He just had it going on! But why would he want to go anywhere with her? Danita did not consider herself to have low self-esteem but honestly in this day and time; white guys didn't date black girls. She knew she looked good, but she also knew she had principles that many girls nowadays were not exercising. One that had proven to be the most problematic was her belief in no premarital sex. Even if he was new to the school that seemed to be common knowledge for all the guys, which is why no one hardly approached her Danita had not realized she had been standing there for quite some time in a daze. Jeremy asked her again, and she quickly replied, "I'm sorry I thought you were talking to my friend," trying to play it off.

Jeremy told her, "I know I don't know you, and you don't know me. I have seen you around, but I was nervous about saying anything to you until my friend convinced me to ask you. So, if you don't have a date, would you like to go to the prom with me?"

"Yes, I will go to the prom with you," she answered, wondering why it took her so long to get it out. They exchanged phone numbers, and Jeremy told Danita he would call her in two days to make further arrangements.

Jeremy was true to his word and called two days later. Danita was ecstatic! He told her that his dad was going to let him use his brand-new Shelby Mustang that dinner would be a surprise. He wanted her to be ready by 6:30 p.m. and to find a sky-blue dress since that was his favorite color.

It seemed like it took forever for prom to come. Nevertheless, it was finally here, and Danita wanted to make the best of it. She had gotten her hair and nails done, and her mom gave her one hundred dollars to buy her dress. It was a strapless, knee-length, sky blue sequence dress that accentuated all her curves. She also made sure that the ground rules were set way before they went any further with their plans. They were only going for a good time, to dance, see their friends, and absolutely no sex! It amazed Danita that Jeremy did not seem to have a problem with that.

It was 6:45 p.m. and they were on their way to the restaurant. Jeremy had been on time, and they stood around, posing for pictures that her mom insisted on taking. The night went along great. They arrived at the prom around 8:30 p.m. She really enjoyed herself that night. They danced, mingled with friends, and got to know each other better.

Danita learned that Jeremy was a native of Atlanta and had just turned nineteen years old. His parents were still married, and after graduation, he was planning on working with his father at his construction company. Danita told him about her upbringing. She was from Atlanta also, and she was about to turn eighteen years old in another two months. She was not sure what she wanted to do after high school. She told him how her mom and dad would fight a lot when she was little. She remembered walking down the street with her mom in the middle of the night with bags in their hands because her mom was leaving her dad. This was the last time she saw him.

Her curfew was 1 a.m., but Jeremy wanted to get her home early so he could make a good impression. He walked her to the front door at 12:45 and gave her a kiss on the cheek. She was a little irritated because she wanted a kiss on the lips, but she was also relieved because it showed that he understood and respected the arrangement. She felt good about that. She walked into the house as he pulled off. From then on, Danita and Jeremy were a couple.

After graduation, Jeremy did work construction with his father and had a place of his own. Danita was working at Southern Bell and was still living with her mom. Since things were going so well, they decided to move in together. A decision she would soon regret. Jeremy insisted they get a joint checking account, but he was the only one with access to the money. If Danita needed money for any reason, she had to ask Jeremy. He would give her a list of things she could get at the grocery store, and everything she brought home had to be from that list.

Danita knew she had a good man that only had a temper when she pushed the wrong buttons. She tried her best to make sure everything was perfect so there would be no issues, but of course, that was impossible. They had been dating for two years and living together for one of those years when the abuse started. The mental abuse started six months prior. It seemed as if she could do nothing right. Jeremy even started alienating her from friends and family.

One night, Jeremy came home drunk from hanging out with his friends, fussing and yelling because dinner wasn't done yet. Danita had just finished making the last of the dinner and was taking the biscuits out of the oven. She assured him that she was in the process of making his plate and to have a seat, and it would be ready. He grabbed her arm so tight that she winced in pain. He let go and sat down at the table. Danita brought him his plate, and as she was setting it down on the table, he pushed her to the floor. She covered her face in preparation for what she feared would happen next.

There was food all over her and the floor. Jeremy knelt with his fist in her face and demanded that she tell him the truth. She thought that he had finally lost it. Tell him the truth about what? When did he bring something up? Was it when he pushed her down? Did she blackout and did not realize it? What was he talking about? Jeremy finally got it out; he said that one of his friends told him that Danita had come onto him and that they had sex. He was getting more and more furious the more he talked. Trying to talk through her tears, Danita told him that it was not true. That she was still a virgin and he knew that, but he had made up his mind and was going to believe his friend no matter what she said.

Jeremy grabbed Danita by her long, wavy black hair and dragged her over to the counter where she kept the silverware. He pulled out one of her butcher knives and told her that she was going to 'give it up' that night or he would slit her throat! Danita was terrified; she didn't know what to think. Should she try to run? What should she do? While she was trying to think of a plan, Jeremy was dragging her to the kitchen table. He picked her up, threw her on the table, and held the knife to her throat, telling her that if she tried to run, he would kill her. Danita cried and shut her eyes as tight as she could thinking that maybe this was all a bad dream and she would wake up, and this wouldn't be happening. Jeremy violated her all the while cursing at her because he felt she had him waiting for way too long. He kept saying how patient he had been, and how he didn't understand why she would have sex with his friend but not him. Danita was in excruciating pain. What felt like forever was only a matter of minutes. She kept her eyes closed until Jeremy was done. He staggered over to the couch and collapsed. Danita laid there for a second not sure what to do, think, or say. She was trying to comprehend what had just happened. She heard this aggravating noise and realized it was Jeremy snoring.

She realized if she was ever going to get away from him, this would be the time. She rolled herself off the table clutching the shreds of clothes she was still wearing. She was in so much pain she could barely walk. Danita stumbled over to the table stand next to the door, grabbed her purse, and her keys. She looked back one more time to make sure Jeremy was still on the couch, and with a deep sigh, she opened the door gently and walked out. She could not believe she was actually doing this. Danita got in the car and drove to the hospital, which was the last place she wanted to go because she could not stand hospitals. She explained to the nurse what had happened, and the doctors ran their tests. They also had to do a rape kit. At that point, Danita was so uncomfortable she was not even sure if she should have gone through with all of it. The doctor called the police; she gave her statement and pressed charges. Danita overheard the police officers talking to the doctor about how they despised doing domestic violence cases on black women because their bruises were not always as evident, which makes the cases harder to try in court. The doctor seemed to take forever to come back into the room. She came back with the results from the X-rays. She explained to Danita what she saw on the X-ray and why she was in so much pain. She had two broken ribs and a dislocated jaw.

Three years later Danita and her son Germaine moved back in with her mother in Atlanta. Jeremy was in jail for rape, which was his second offense, and aggravated assault with a deadly weapon. Danita had changed jobs. She was working for NationsBank and had made assistant manager at her branch. It was a lot of pressure on her, but she liked the job, and the people she worked with were a lot of fun.

One day when the bank was about an hour away from closing, a man came into the bank and caught all the tellers' attention. They were arguing over who was going to help him. A couple of minutes later, the customer started getting loud and yelling. Danita came out of her office to see what was going on. She walked over to the counter, introduced herself as the assistant branch manager, and asked if she could be of assistance. He introduced himself as Paul Smith and started to explain the situation to her. He was trying to get a couple of checks deposited into his account, one of which was for over six thousand dollars. He did not know there would have to be a hold placed on the check to verify the funds. He wanted the money to be readily available. Danita could see that he was getting more and more irritated the more he explained the situation. She took the information from the teller and asked him to step into her office to further discuss the matter.

Almost two hours later, they both came out laughing and talking as if nothing had ever taken place. She had gotten his deposits straightened out and made him understand that it was company policy. They had gotten past the business conversation and started a personal one. He was curious about her, telling her that she was too beautiful not to have a man. Danita informed him of her past situation with Germaine's father and that she was not interested in getting into another relationship. She found it surprising how easy and relaxing it was to talk to him, though. She had not felt comfortable enough to tell her closest co-worker that information, let alone a stranger.

Danita was curious about him, too. Not too many people came into the bank with that amount of money, and from what she saw, he always had a healthy amount of money in his account. He told her that he owned two restaurants, one on the east side of town and another in Savannah, Georgia. Finding out that information intrigued Danita. He had accomplished a lot and didn't look to be older than his mid-thirties. Mr. Paul Smith was not bad on the eyes either. He was tall, at least 6'4, had a goatee, muscular build weighing at least 215 pounds, with a nice smooth mocha complexion, and no ring on his finger.

As he was leaving, he complimented her on her professionalism in dealing with his situation, and how she did a very good job of calming him down, which was not an easy task when it came to his money. Danita walked him to the door, unlocked and opened it to let him out.

Paul stopped, turned around, and asked, "do you have plans tonight? I just got back into town from visiting my other restaurant and would love to go to dinner with you after you finish up here."

Danita felt like her face was bright red. She hesitated and tried to keep the professionalism that he just complimented her on when she replied, "I have a rule about dating my customers as I feel it is a complete conflict of interest and besides if it doesn't work out, it tends to make things a little awkward."

"Well, I guess I will have to cancel my account; that way there are no excuses."

"Paul, that wouldn't be right. We can't have you cancel your account over something so minuscule." She went on to express how much the bank appreciated his business.

He could not go on with it any longer and started laughing, "I'm sorry, but you should see the look on your face! I'm just messing with you. I wanted to see what your response would be if I threatened to cancel my account."

Danita felt flustered. She did not know whether to be upset with him or laugh. She walked back to her office and grabbed one of her business cards, wrote her home number on it, and then handed it to Paul. She told him while she appreciated the offer, tonight was too short of notice. She reminded him of her young son at home and that she did not have time to find a babysitter.

Paul smiled and told her that he could respect that. He asked when the best time would be to call her. She told him anytime. He had both her home number and work number there on the card. He smiled, took her hand, softly kissed the back of it and told her that he would be going out of town again the day after next, but he would call her as soon as he got back.

A week passed, and Danita still had not heard from Paul Smith. She tried to get him out of her head, but she could not. He had made a big impression on her, and she could not shake it. Two weeks to the day, after they met, she received a phone call at work that made her day.

"Good morning, Danita. I am truly sorry that I have not called you for so long. I just got back into town. My trip took a little longer than I expected. If you allow me to make it up to you, I can take you out to dinner tomorrow night. Do you think that is enough time to get a babysitter? Will I be able to meet your son?"

Danita was happy to hear from him but was also a little irritated, "What makes you think I still want to go out with you? You told me a couple of days, and now here it is two weeks later, and you think I'm just going to go along with your plans, huh? I'm not sure if you can make it up to me. How do I know you don't have a wife in Savannah, and that's why you take so many 'business' trips?"

Paul was truly hurt by her accusations. "I know that you don't know me very well and because you don't, I'm going to let that go. I am not the type of person that cheats or has various wives spread out across the country. Once you get to know me, you will realize that. I honestly apologize that my trip took longer than couple of days, but I didn't want to call you and not be able to talk to you. I didn't think you would appreciate that seeing as how you barely know me, but in the future, I will call you to touch base, is that fair?"

"I'm sorry I blew up on you. At first, I was joking, but I think my real emotions got the best of me. I don't know what it is about you, but you really made an impression on me when we met. Those two weeks were hard. I wanted to hear your voice and I know that sounds crazy because I barely know you, but yes, I feel that is fair."

"I can respect that. I was not going to say anything, but I feel the same way. You do not know how many times I was in Savannah holding meetings with my employees but thinking about you and that beautiful smile. You truly make it hard to stay focused on work. I will make sure that I stay in touch with you whether I am out of town or not."

"Well, if your offer still stands, I would like to go to dinner with you tomorrow night. However, I'm not sure I am ready for you to meet my son just yet."

"I can understand that. Moreover, yes, my offer always stands. I told you I would never pass up a date with you. So how about I pick you up around 6 p.m.?"

"That is fine. Where were you planning on taking me? I mean do I need to dress up or be casual?"

"I want you to dress how you would if you were going to work. I want to take you to someplace special."

"Okay, that's fine. So, I will see you tomorrow at six?"

"Definitely."

"Good-bye Paul," Danita said.

"Good-bye, Ms. Williams. You have a good day, and I look forward to seeing you tomorrow."

Danita did not think Saturday night would come soon enough, but it was 5:30 and she had nothing but butterflies. It had been three years since she went on a date. She was looking forward to it and was nervous at the same time. She changed clothes at least ten times. She always received compliments at work on how well she dressed, but for some reason today, she could not find anything to wear. She finally picked out a red blouse, a white blazer, a white skirt, and red pumps with gold accessories. It was 5:50 when the doorbell rang. She took one last look in the mirror, put on her pumps, and hurried to the door. By the time she got there, her mom had already let him in and was giving him the third degree.

"Hello Paul, how are you doing?" Danita asked, trying to contain her excitement.

"I'm great now that I have seen you," he said as he reached down and gave her a peck on the cheek. "You look remarkable! I wasn't sure if it was appropriate or not, but I bought you a present." He handed her a wrapped box with a ribbon on it.

Danita opened the gift. It was a beautiful set of pearl earrings. She immediately took her earrings off and replaced them with the new set. She was ecstatic as she walked to the mirror to model them.

"Thank you, Paul. They are beautiful, and they go perfectly with this outfit, but you really didn't have to."

"You don't have to thank me. I saw them in the jewelry store and knew they would look great on you."

"That is quite an expensive gift, isn't it, Paul?" Danita's mom questioned, giving him a suspicious look.

"No ma'am it wasn't all that expensive, but even if it were, I believe your daughter is worth every penny I have and more."

Danita decided to get him out of the house before her mom could start in on her six-hour quiz session.

"Paul are you ready to go?" she asked, reaching for his hand.

"Yes, I am. I made a reservation at the restaurant; I wouldn't want us to be late."

"Bye mother," Danita touched her mom on the shoulder, giving her a kiss on the cheek, "I will see you later."

"Good-bye Mrs. Williams, it was really nice meeting you," Paul said while shaking her hand.

"It was nice to meet you too, Paul. For the record, it will go over well if you bring the mom a gift as well," Danita's mom said with a slight grin on her face.

"I will remember that next time," Paul said as they walked out the door. Paul surprised Danita by taking her to his restaurant for dinner.

Danita was lost in her thoughts until she realized her son was talking to her.

"Ma, are you okay? I've been standing here for a good minute; didn't you hear me?" Germaine said.

"Oh, I'm sorry honey I didn't see you standing there I was in deep thought. Where are my beautiful daughter-in-law and my grandbabies?" Danita said while getting up to hug her eldest son.

"They are already in the house. Are you sure you are okay? I have never seen you look that way before. It was as if your body was there, but your mind was somewhere else, and it looks like you've been crying."

"Sweetie I'm okay. I told you I was just thinking about some things. Now let's go in the house so I can see my grandbabies."

Germaine followed his mom in the house, not convinced there was nothing wrong. Danita walked into the veranda where her daughter-in-law and grandchildren were. She could not help but smile at the sight of her babies. They ran into her arms as if this was the first time, they had seen their grandma. They were yelling, "Nana, Nana, we missed you. Do you have any toys for us, Nana?"

Danita answered, laughing at the children, "No, not today, babies."

"What about money, Nana?" The children said in unison.

Danita laughed harder, "No, not this time but you know Christmas is right around the corner? Have you started on your lists?" She asked, still holding the grandkids.

"No, ma'am."

Danita shook her head, "Why don't you go ahead and start on that list, so Nana will know what you want?"

The kids scurried off to find a pen and paper.

"Mom, you spoil them, you know that, right?" Germaine asked as he sat down next to his wife, Jennifer.

They were sitting around talking, and the children started playing hide and seek when the doorbell rang. Germaine went to answer it, and his siblings bombarded him as he opened the door. It was his brothers, Chris and his family, Anthony and his family, and his baby sister Marie and her children. It had been so long since he last saw his brothers and sister. He looked at them and relished in the moment, and then he rushed them all for a huge bear hug. Anthony is the tallest out of all the men at 6'5.

Danita asked her daughters-in-law to help her set the table while Marie arranged the food. Danita was so happy to see all her children and grandchildren. Once Marie arranged everything, Danita asked Germaine to say the prayer for the family. All the adults were at the big table and the children at the kiddies' table. Everyone was talking about old times and eating as if they had not eaten in years.

After the men ate, they piled into the family room to watch football on the big flat screen TV. Danita loved times like these where all her family was present and enjoying each other's company. Everyone started packing up to leave, gathering all their things, and making to-go plates about 8 p.m. They finally left about an hour later.

Danita walked around the house, ensuring all the outside lights were on, and the doors were locked. She set the alarm all the while reminiscing on how great today had been. She really enjoyed seeing her family and always vowed to get together more often, but it never seemed to work out. Danita thought holidays were never enough. Her children took quite a bit of the food, and what was left over, she went ahead and separated. Since it was just her, she set some aside for the week and froze the remaining. Danita was tired and headed to bed. She was trying to get to sleep but could not stop thinking about the past, the letter she received from Jeremy, and her late husband. Tears fell from her eyes as she thought about her late husband, Paul.

Paul and Danita dated for about two years before getting married. Paul was a Christian and very devoted to his faith, so it was never necessary for her to bring up anything contrary to the Bible. As a matter of fact, Paul told Danita after six months of dating that he planned to marry her. He wanted to be sure they lived according to the Word, so there would be no sex before marriage. He wanted to make sure they connected emotionally and spiritually. Danita appreciated that. They had a small intimate wedding at the home he had built for them; it was a dream come true. Danita pulled out their wedding album flipped through each page reminiscing at each moment.

2.

GERMAINE & JENNIFER

It had started to rain on the way home. Germaine needed to stop off at the gas station to get gas as well as a pack of gum since he left his at home. He got out of the car and peeked back in to ask Jennifer if she wanted anything, she shook her head no, and he walked into the store.

Jennifer watched as her husband went into the Quik-E Mart. She could not help but smile at how gorgeous he was. Germaine was about 6'2 with a light caramel complexion and weighed about 210 pounds. He sported a goatee and a bald head. He was a 'pretty boy' to the T. She loved him for his great personality. He knew what he wanted out of life, he was determined to reach his goal, and he was a great provider.

She tried to let her mind drift, but she could not help it. Jennifer could not stand going over to Danita's house. She felt so much tension when she went over there. She was convinced Germaine's family did not like her. Nevertheless, every time she tried to discuss this with Germaine, it led to an argument. Jennifer just could not understand why he did not see this for himself. The night was so nice she felt the subject was not worth mentioning. She did not want to hear it, not tonight.

Germaine returned to the burgundy Chevrolet Suburban XLT loaner that he received while the auto shop worked on his Mercedes Benz. He was already chewing the gum that he bought. "What's wrong honey? You look like you have something on your mind."

"Nothing Maine, I'm okay, just a little tired. I am ready to get home and get in the bed. You know some people do have to go to work in the morning." Jennifer said with a slight giggle.

"I have told you a thousand times that you don't have to work. In fact, I believe I told you that you could stop working. You know the accounting firm brings in more than enough money. There's no reason for you to have to work as far as money is concerned," Germaine said as he pulled out of the parking lot.

"I know I don't have to work. I know the business brings in more than enough money, but you know how I am; I just must be around people. If I don't, I will drive myself crazy. I'm a people person, and working is the best place for me right now." She replied while rubbing his inner thigh.

Germaine started to smile, "You know I like that. You're gonna get something started in this car if you keep that up."

"First of all, I know how much you like that, but I also know that nothing is getting started in this car with two kids in the back," Jennifer said through her laughter.

"Well, we can carry it on into the house. I mean we don't have to do it right here, but it would be nice to do something spontaneous occasionally. We are starting to get so predictable. Remember when we got married how spontaneous we were. We used to just get up and go. We need to get back into doing that. You know it helps keeps marriages alive."

"So, you think our marriage is boring?" Jennifer asked, trying not to reveal how hurt she was by her husband's insinuation.

"No baby, our marriage is anything but boring."

"Well, why do you think we need to be more spontaneous? We do things together."

"Do you remember when we first got married? Even though we had CJ, it was like we made more time for us than just staying at home and working all the time."

"I remember, in the first year we were married we took two trips and a cruise. You have always shown me different things and different places. It was beautiful, and I would love to do that again, but now that we have children, it's not as easy to just pick up and go." "I don't' understand why not. We can do a quick little weekend getaway. Let my mom watch the boys one weekend and just go. Then we could take another vacation and bring the boys with us. Baby, I just miss spending time with you. Don't get me wrong, I love being with the kids and spending time with them also, but parents need time by themselves too, you know."

"I know, and if you really want to go somewhere, we can do that. Where do you want to go?" She asked, feeling herself getting excited.

"I thought you would never ask! I've been looking at some great brochures, and I have narrowed it down to a three-day-two-night cruise to the Bahamas, or we could go to Vegas, you know we have never been there. What do you think?" Germaine was ecstatic. He was finally going to be able to go on a vacation with his beautiful wife, just the two of them and he could not wait. He loved to see his wife on the beach in her bikini. He loved his wife, and all he wanted was the chance to show her how much she meant to him.

"The thought of being on another cruise with you on the beach sounds very promising," Jennifer said. She leaned over and kissed Germaine on the cheek.

"What was that for?"

"That was for being a wonderful husband and caring enough about our marriage to want to keep it exciting. I mean some men wouldn't even want to take the initiative to make the marriage more exciting or anything like that. The first thing they think about is cheating or trying to find it somewhere else. It really means a lot to me."

"Why wouldn't I want our marriage to work? Baby, when I took my vows to love, honor, and cherish you for the rest of my life, that is what I intend to do. I take my vows very seriously. I would do anything in my power to keep you happy and keep this marriage going. I love you, I love our kids, and first and foremost, I love God, and He keeps me in line."

Jennifer adjusted herself in her seat so that she could face Germaine while she spoke to him. She looked in the backseat to check on the boys, who were fast asleep. "Do you remember when we first met?"

"Of course, I remember."

"It was the summer of '02, and I was working as a receptionist for Seymour and Cain Accounting. You had just started working there. The first time I saw you, I remember thinking how fine you were. You probably thought I didn't see all those times you were looking at me, but I did. I could not understand why it took you so long to ask me out. When you finally asked me out, I was so happy. It was the Friday of 4th of July weekend, and we were just about to close the office when you pulled me aside and asked me what my plans were. You invited me and CJ to your mom's house for that wonderful barbecue. The food was so good, and I still cannot get over the fact that she cooked all that food by herself!

It surprised me that you wanted to date me even though you knew I had a child; most men would have dipped. You stayed and treated him as if he was yours.

Within those years we dated I never believed I could be any happier until the day you proposed to me. I was already proud of you for opening your own practice. For you to propose, meant that you wanted me to be a part of it also, you just don't know how happy that made me. After we were married and I had Benjamin, I saw the look in your eyes from having your own son; I wanted to give you that much happiness every day of your life. I love you, Germaine, forever and always." She leaned in and kissed him on the cheek.

"I love you too, baby. You know that day that you had Benjamin, that look in my eyes was not because he was my son, it was because I love you so much and you had just gone through an extraordinary experience. I wished I could have been there for you when you had CJ. I would have enjoyed being there with you when you had him too. You were so beautiful and serene, no matter how much you yelled and screamed and called me names," Germaine chuckled.

Jennifer laid her head on her husband's shoulder as he drove the remainder of the way home. She closed her eyes and went to sleep.

"Wake up honey, we're home," Germaine said gently kissing her on the forehead.

"We're home already. How long was I sleep?" Jennifer stretched and let out a long yawn.

"About an hour."

If anything was good about going over his mom's house, it was the length of time it took to get home since they lived in Alpharetta.

Germaine and Jennifer exited the Suburban and started getting the children out. She led the boys into the house, got them into bed while Germaine closed the garage, and locked up for the night.

He walked across the hall toward the master bedroom and stopped to look out over the banister. Sometimes he just enjoyed standing there taking in the view. His wife decorated the house with such exquisite taste. It gave that relaxing, calm feel. Jennifer had convinced him that lavender would look good in the living room and he had to admit she was right. They had a white leather sectional couch with an armrest in the middle that had a built-in remote, cup holders, and settings for a massage and recliner that he had custom-built. She had a massive family portrait on the wall. The walls were a sponged mixture of lavender and white, and that set everything into its correct place.

Germaine walked into the bedroom and saw his wife in her walk-in closet changing her clothes. She was beautiful. He loved her long wavy red hair that stopped just above her waistline, and her skin was silky smooth like milk. She had an hourglass figure and green almond-shaped eyes. "Did you enjoy yourself over mom's house?" he asked, wrapping his long arms around her small frame.

'Here we go,' Jennifer thought, 'why do we have to go through this?' Why can't he just leave that subject alone?' "It was okay," she sighed heavily, not wanting to get on this subject again.

"Why just okay? Did something happen?" Germaine asked while getting undressed in his closet.

"Baby I really do not want to talk about it right now? Can we please just go to bed and talk about this later?"

"Why don't you want to talk about it? It wasn't that bad, was it? Was the food, okay?" Germaine stepped out of his closet, staring at his wife with a look of concern.

"Everything was fine, just like it always is. I'm the only one who senses the tension. It is always me; like you did not notice the stares and the evil eyes from your family. I might not have gone to college and graduated top of my class, but I am very intelligent. And I hate that they make me feel like I am not."

There was silence in the room. Jennifer grabbed her pajamas, instead of the sexy lingerie she had planned to wear, hastily put them on, and climbed into bed. "So, are you just going to act like you didn't hear me, or are you just not going to respond?"

"What do you want me to say? You always do this after we come back from my mom's house. If it is not one thing, it's another. They did not talk to you, or they gave you evil looks. It is almost as if you don't want them to like you." Germaine said, annoyed.

"So, because I always say it, does that make it less credible? I think you don't want to believe your family can have any flaws." Jennifer said, getting very irritated.

"You are taking what I am saying out of context," Germaine said as he was walking around to his side of the bed to get under the covers. He had removed his clothes and always preferred to sleep in boxers.

"Maine, your family does not like me. They barely even look at me without giving some kind of glare. I don't know how much longer I can take this," she said almost in tears.

"Jennifer, baby, I think you are over-reacting. My family loves you and always has. The only thing they had a problem with was the fact that you already had a child when we got together. You know they are old-fashioned. Nevertheless, they have come to terms with that and have moved on. Now they love you and both kids. Things are fine if you give it a chance and stop believing they are out to get you."

Jennifer jumped out of bed to face Germaine, "It's easy for you to say. They are your family! I guess that is why you do not see it. We have been married for almost eight years now; you would think they would have gotten used to the idea of me already having a child before we got married if that is the real reason."

"Why wouldn't that be the real reason? What else could it be?" Germaine was honestly confused.

Jennifer tried to leave the room. She almost made it to the door, but Germaine jumped up, ran over, and grabbed her arm, "we have to finish this conversation. You know I do not like to go to bed when we are both upset. I would like answers to my questions."

Jennifer attempted to snatch her arm away, but his grip was too strong. She glared into his eyes with a look of contempt and hurt.

"Germaine, I believe your family does not like me because I'm white. I've told you this before'."

Germaine let go of her arm, "So you're saying my family is racist?"

"I don't know, but I really don't think it has anything to do with CJ. I believe it is because of the color of my skin. I mean, think about it. How many white people are in your family?"

"No, we don't have any other white people in our family, but my parents have always told us that they do not care who we bring home as long as they have our same morals and values. They have always been supportive. I've dated outside my race before. You are the only one who has ever said they felt like it was a problem."

"I don't want to talk about this tonight. I do not want to go through this again."

Germaine looked at Jennifer. He watched in disbelief as she put some clothes in an overnight bag. Germaine put his hands on his head as if that would stop all the cruel thoughts that were going through his head. He stroked his temples then looked at his wife again. He walked over to his side of the bed.

He finally spoke, "You don't really intend to leave in the middle of the night, do you?"

"Germaine, I love you, but I can't deal with this situation right now. And for you to just sit there and pretend that it doesn't exist hurts me more than anything."

"So, you want to leave because I don't think my family has prejudiced feelings for you and you think they do?"

"No, I need time to figure things out. Maine, I love you so much, but I really need some time" Jennifer said, her head hung low.

"What are you talking about? What was all that talk in the car not too long ago? Have you forgotten about that? Or was that an act?" Germaine was fuming beyond comprehension. He wanted to storm out of the house and scream to the top of his lungs or hit her; whichever one came first, but he figured since he does not hit women and he wants to hear an explanation he might as well stay there and listen to what she had to say.

"It was not an act. I love you! I need to get my mind right and figure out why this aggravates me so much. I need space. I really need you to allow me this time to come correct." Jennifer said while trying to push back tears.

"Okay, you need time, that's fine. Why can't you just sleep in one of the other bedrooms? Why do you need to leave the house to have your space?" He asked, trying to get a grasp on it.

"Maine, I know this is probably not making sense to you. Just look at it like this; me being in the same house is not giving me space. I need time away from the house, you, and the kids so I can think. I am overwhelmed right now, and I need this!"

"Okay, I tell you what. Why don't you go to the beach house in Malibu? That way, you will have time away from us, you can get your head right, and maybe you will be able to really talk about what is going on." Germaine said while reaching out to his wife.

Jennifer walked over to her husband with tears and a smile on her face. She told him that it was a good idea and gave him a hug and a kiss. She walked over to the kids' room. She kissed them both on the cheek and left.

Germaine paced his bedroom, trying to understand what just took place. In one instance, he wanted to run after her, bring her back, and tell her that they could work through this. Then again, why should he? She had told him she needed some space and he wanted to give it to her. Does this mean she didn't love him anymore? Was this what he should have done? Why would he give her space? Is there someone else? Germaine was so enraged he picked up a crystal vase that he had given Jennifer on their third wedding anniversary, raised it over his head ready to throw it as if that would solve all his problems when Benjamin walked into the room. It was at that moment Germaine realized no matter how mad he was, he had to keep his cool, especially since he was going to be there taking care of the boys for an unspecified amount of time. Germaine replaced the vase, slowly walked over to Ben and put his hand on his shoulder, "What's wrong little man? I thought you were sleeping."

"I heard some loud noises that woke me up," Ben said groggily while rubbing his eyes trying to focus.

Germaine picked him up and gave him the biggest hug he had ever given. He put him in their huge king-sized bed, covered him up, and kissed him on the head.

He needed to vent. He needed to talk to someone. Who could he call? He definitely couldn't talk to his brothers because he knew what they would say, 'I told you about her man. You should have listened to me. I don't even know why you trippin' you don't need to be with her no ways.' How could they be so shallow? He wanted to call his mother. Germaine knew that although she had given her suspicions about Jennifer in the past, that she would not judge and would be objective to the situation. He picked up the phone and started dialing her number when he happened to look at the clock. It was one o'clock in the morning. Germaine placed the phone back on the receiver, climbed back into bed, and watched his son sleeping peacefully until tears started to burn his eyes. He couldn't hold them back any longer.

That night Germaine cried himself to sleep.

3.

CHRISTOPHER & JUANITA

Chris pulled his Lexus LS400 into the driveway, stopped at the gate, entered the code, and waited for it to open. He pulled up to his four-story all brick estate in Powder Springs. Every time he came home, he just had to reflect on how fortunate he was. Juanita escorted the children inside to get them ready for bed. Chris stayed outside to look at the swan fountain in the middle of the circular driveway. It was so breathtaking.

He considered himself to be a very successful corporate lawyer with handsome ten-year-old twin boys, John and Justin, and a beautiful wife of twelve years. Yep, he was unquestionably blessed. After taking it all in, Chris went into his home and headed straight for the wet bar in his office, which was a part of his everyday routine. His wife cannot stand that he drinks every day, but as he explained to her, "he just drinks to unwind from the hectic day." He is not an alcoholic, and he can stop at any time, but why would he want to?

Juanita came down the stairs to see what was taking Chris so long. She had just tucked the boys into bed and was ready to get into bed herself. This was becoming part of her nightly routine, she thought. She tucked the boys in and then searched the entire house trying to find her husband. She sleeps better at night when Chris is there beside her. Lately, Juanita hasn't had to go around the whole house to locate him because he has been in the same room for the past few months, his office, having a drink. Juanita could not stand to see her husband drink so much, mainly because her father was an alcoholic. He would get drunk and then fight with her mom. She couldn't wait to be old enough to leave that life behind. Juanita did have to admit that there is a huge difference between Chris and her dad. Chris is very educated and has always taken care of his household. Her husband may drink every day, but he only has about one or two shots of Hennessy or Courvoisier but never enough to get drunk. She had to give him his props for that.

"There you are beau," Juanita said as she stood in the doorway taking in all his handsomeness. Chris has a beautiful dark brown complexion with a mustache, a low hair cut with black hair and spots of gray at the top; he stood about 6'3 and weighed 230 pounds.

"Here I am, b-a-b-y," Chris said in a melodic tone. "Come to Papi and tell me all about your day."

Juanita laughed and tried to look serious as she sat on his lap. "What do you mean tell you about my day? I have been with you all day!"

"Yeah, but you are looking good in them shorts. I haven't seen that all day." Chris was eyeing his wife by now and staring her down like she was a piece of succulent ribeye steak. She was wearing his favorite pair of pajamas. He loved seeing his wife in them. The pajama top was a white tank top, and the shorts were pink boy shorts. Her smooth, caramel skin just seemed to accentuate it even more.

'She knows these drive me crazy,' he thought.

"So," Juanita said with her arms wrapped around her husband's neck, "What time are you planning on going to bed?"

"What time you want me to go to bed?" Chris asked, already knowing the answer. He slowly ran his finger up and down her spine. He knew this drove her crazy. Juanita softly kissed her husband's lips. She abruptly stopped.

"What's wrong?" Chris asked.

"I forgot you've been drinking. I can't stand the taste of alcohol on your breath. It's such a turn-off." Juanita was irritated. She got up and started walking towards the stairs.

"Umm, are you kidding me right now? We have kissed plenty of times after I've had something to drink. It's never bothered you before! Why now?"

Chris felt himself getting angry as he followed his wife up the stairs with a drink in hand.

"Maybe so Chris but I told you numerous times about my past and how my dad used to drink. You know how much it gets under my skin. I don't want to be around that. I'm in no way comparing you to my father, but I know what alcohol can lead to. I don't want to see you go down that road." They had reached the top of the stairs at this point. Juanita put her hand on Chris' cheek and caressed it.

"I'm glad you feel I'm nothing like your father. You know I don't drink that often. Yes, when I do, I go in, but I can stop at any time." Chris said as he hugged his wife.

"Okay, if you are really serious that you can stop at any time, then, prove it to me by pouring out that drink in your hand. If you can accomplish that, then we can slowly work on getting rid of that stash you have downstairs in your office." Juanita pulled away and looked up at him.

"Woman you trippin' and must have bumped yo head! Do you know how much money I spent on that alcohol down there? And you want me to throw it out? Uh no," Chris said as he walked past Juanita headed towards the bedroom.

"Okay well. Just pour out the drink in your hand. Start with that. If you won't throw it out. I'm sleeping in the guest bedroom tonight and every night until you do."

Chris watched his wife storm down the hall, grab her stuff from their bedroom, and head to the guest room. He could not believe she was about to turn this into an argument again. He could not understand why she continuously got upset about his drinking. She's even admitted that he is nothing like her father, so why make a big deal of it. Chris sighed in disgust. He was getting tired of the drama as they seem to go through this at least once a week. He went back downstairs, into his office and took the top off his small bottle of Hennessey. He downed the whole bottle in less than a few seconds. He decided; he might as well get it all in while he had the opportunity.

 "Let's see who comes begging who. I know she can't sleep unless I'm in bed with her." Chris said aloud to himself with a slight grin. "She'll come around." He grabbed a half a bottle of Patron Silver. headed to their bedroom, plopped on the bed, drunk the rest of the tequila, and fell asleep.

4.

ANTHONY & DANIELLE

Danielle pulled their Audi into the garage; everyone got out the vehicle and made their way into the house. Anthony went around their 2,800 square foot ranch-style home, making sure everything was locked and turning the lights off while Danielle put their son to bed. They met up in the hallway and headed to the bedroom hand in hand. Anthony sat down on their recliner. Danielle sat down on Anthony's lap. Just as they started to kiss their son knocked on the door. "Mommy, I can't sleep. Why is your door locked?" Bradley asked, trying to open their door. Danielle kissed Anthony as she got up to tend to Bradley when the phone rang.

Anthony snatched the phone off the hook in frustration, "Hello."

"What's up, man? Can I speak to Danielle?" A deep male voice answered.

"Who's calling?" Anthony asked with an attitude.

"Yeah folk, my fault; this is Mike."

"Hold on for a minute," Anthony put the phone down, went into his son's room and pulled Danielle out by her arm.

"What in the world is wrong with you? Are you crazy? Don't you ever grab me like that again, especially not in front of our son," Danielle said lividly while pointing her finger in Anthony's face.

"Who in the world is Mike?!" Anthony shouted back.

Danielle looked at him like she'd seen a ghost. How did he know about Mike? She thought.

"The only Mike I know is a co-worker. Why?"

"If he's a co-worker, then why does he have our number? You need to get on the phone right now and tell that negro not to call my house again!" Anthony said.

Anthony went into Bradley's room to make sure he didn't hear all the shouting. Danielle waited until Anthony was in the room, then she ran to the phone and answered, "How did you get my number?"

"Baby don't be like that. You know that's no way to greet your man," Mike said.

"Mike, stop playing games! I don't know what your problem is, but you have got to leave me alone. My husband is going to get the wrong idea about us if you keep this up. I have asked you as nicely as possible to leave me alone, but if this continues, then I will be forced to get a restraining order against you or go to Human Resources. Do you understand?" Danielle was stern trying to make sure that even if Anthony had been listening, he wouldn't get this twisted.

"You know you are so cute when you try to play hard to get. Don't worry. I get the hint. I'll call you at a better time or just see you at work tomorrow." Mike hung up before she could reply.

Danielle awoke to the sound of Whitney Houston's 'I Will Always Love You' playing on her radio alarm clock. She turned it off, got out of bed, and groggily walked to the bathroom. She brushed her teeth. 'Can't kiss hubby with stank breath.' She laughed at herself. She came out of the bathroom ready to plant a big wet one her husband since they were interrupted last night. She hated when they argued. She made her way to the king-sized canopy bed, flipped on the lamp, and saw that her husband was not there.

She was confused. 'It's only 6:15 in the morning. Where could he be?' She went to the guest bedroom to see if he was asleep in there. She realized the bed hadn't been slept in. She went to Bradley's room to get him ready for school, but he was not there either. She started to panic, not sure of where her son or her husband was. She immediately started calling their names while checking every room until she came to the kitchen and noticed a note Anthony left.

Sorry, I didn't wake you, but I had to go to work early this morning. I wanted to let you get a little more sleep, so

I took Bradley to daycare. Hope I didn't alarm you. I know how quickly you can get concerned. I love you, and I will call you after my meetings.

Love Anthony

Danielle breathed a sigh of relief, not sure what had gone through her mind as to the whereabouts of her family, but she was elated to know they were alright. She was startled by the ringing of the phone and just knew it was Anthony calling to tell her he loved her despite their argument the night before.

"Hello."

"Hello, baby. I wasn't sure if you would be up yet. But I needed to hear your beautiful voice to get me going."

"Mike! What in the world do you want? And why are you calling me? I thought I made it very clear last night not to call me! Why can't you just leave me alone?" Danielle screamed into the phone, disappointed that it wasn't her husband and frustrated with this situation. She was tired of the phone calls, the flowers on her desk and him always being around her at work. This was becoming too much!

"Well, you know I saw your husband leave this morning, so I figured the coast was clear. Are you telling me that you don't want to talk to me? Can I come up?"

"You're finally getting the point. No, I don't want to talk to you. No, you can't come in! I don't want you calling my number again, and if you do, I will get a restraining order on you!"

"Oh, so it's like that, huh? All I want to know is why you broke it off?"

"Mike, we were never together. We barely speak at work. Why would you think something was going on with us?"

"I know what I know. You can't tell me that one night didn't mean anything to you. You said you were going to be with me. I don't understand you. I am not going to leave you alone until you explain to me what happened."

Danielle was almost in tears. She had completely forgotten about that night. "How could you think we would be together? Obviously, you don't remember that night as much as you think you do, and it hurts me to know that I didn't do anything about it. Maybe if I did, you would be in jail now and not harassing me."

Danielle sat down at her dining room table, not sure if she really wanted to go over the circumstances of that night. 'She had made bad decisions before, but if only she had decided to go home instead of having another drink, it would have never happened.' She thought.

"Hello, Elle, you still there?"

Danielle hadn't realized she was still holding the phone and slammed it down on the receiver. She immediately ran to her room, got dressed, and called her job to let them know she wasn't coming in.

'I have to talk to Anthony about that night. I pray he forgives me for not telling him before,' she thought as she went to the garage to warm up her Ford Expedition.

'Oh, my goodness,' she thought aloud. 'What if he doesn't believe me? What if he leaves me over this stupid mistake? I should have just told him the truth last night. I cannot talk myself out of this; he has to know.'

Danielle went into the guest bathroom to make sure she was decent, swooped her hair up into a ponytail, grabbed her purse, picked up her cell phone, made sure it was on and dropped it in her purse. She remembered what Mike said that she seemed not to catch onto before. "I saw your husband leave this morning." That means he was outside the house watching. She ran to the alarm system, punched in the code, and was out the door.

"I hate this subdivision! It has way too many turns," Danielle said angrily while making a left onto Wilshire Street. She came to a stop sign and made a left as she noticed a vehicle speeding towards her. The vehicle slammed into her driver side knocking her unconscious.

5.

MARIE

"Byron, you get in bed right now, or you are getting a spanking! Derek, you have been in that bathtub long enough. Wash up and get to bed!" Marie didn't understand why she had to go through the same routine with these boys every night. They knew what they were supposed to do. Why do they act like this is their first time hearing me say this? Is it punishment? Did I do this to my mom when I was growing up? Lord, I hope not. Marie was putting up the leftover food from her mom's house when the phone rang. They had gotten home about twenty minutes prior. She loved her ranch. Her home was not as big as her brothers, but she felt it was big enough for their family. Marie decorated it herself and done a great job if she said so herself. It is a three bedroom two and a half bath ranch style home with a two-car garage.

She rushed to the phone, "Hello."

"Hey, sweetie. Did I wake you?" Danita asked almost in a whisper.

"No, Ma. I'm just putting up the leftovers and then headed to bed. What's up?" Marie said as she walked back to the food.

"You were on my mind, so I wanted to call you before I went to bed. Is everything okay? Are you good?" Danita was genuinely concerned. She knows how difficult the holidays are for her.

"Ma, thank you for calling; today was difficult for me. I'm not going to lie, but I'm trying to manage. How are you?" Marie said as her eyes began to swell with tears.

"I'm okay. I was just thinking about your father and looking through the photo album. I know he would have enjoyed today." Danita was crying as well.

"Yes, I know, Mom. They both would have enjoyed today. Does this get any easier? I mean Brad has been gone for six months. It feels like it was just yesterday. It still feels so fresh, so raw, so difficult."

"I know sweetie. When your father passed, it took a long time for me to heal – to cope. I know what you are feeling. It's just going to take time. Please know that I am here for you if you ever need to talk. But, honestly, God is going to be your refuge. He is going to be your comforter. He is the only one that can bring you peace that surpasses all understanding. You will need to lean on Him to bring you strength. God is the only reason I was able to keep going, to wake up every morning, to continue taking care of my children; He gave me strength." Danita had stopped crying by now as she was encouraging herself by encouraging her daughter.

"I know. I know you are right. I did see how strong you were after dad died. I just could not believe it. It didn't occur to me that it was because of your faith and prayer. Thank you for the call tonight, mama. I didn't realize how much I needed it. I love you!"

Marie wiped the tears from her eyes and finished putting up the leftovers.

"I love you too, baby. I hear my grandbabies in the background. I'm going to let you go so you can get them in the bed. Are we still going shopping in the morning?"

"You know, I completely forgot about that. I'm not really feeling the Black Friday shopping this year."

"Well, I found some really good sales at Macy's and Target. If you decide to go, let me know. I will be up at 4 a.m."

"Okay, mama," Marie said chuckling, shaking her head. She knows her mom loves to shop, especially if it's a good deal. That's one thing they can count on no matter how old they get; her mom still shops for all of them. "I will let you know. Goodnight, Mom."

"Goodnight, baby. Sleep tight."

Marie went to her bedroom and changed her clothes. She looked at Brad's closet. She had not been in there since he died. Marie took a deep breath and went inside. She grabbed a box and started folding up his clothes. She grabbed another box from the top shelf that she did not recognize. She opened it and dumped the contents on the floor. Marie sat down and went through the items. Among the contents was an unmarked videotape. She went over to her media console, put the tape in the VCR, and pressed play. Marie could not understand what she was watching. It was so confusing especially since there were no markings on the videotape and no date on the screen. It was Brad with another woman and a little boy. It was a home video of them opening Christmas presents.

6.

JENNIFER

Jennifer dizzily wiped her eyes as she awoke out of the elegant, soft, plush bed in the master bedroom of their Malibu home. The view has always been beautiful there. She put on her robe and walked over to the balcony and let the scene consume her. She had been there for two days, and it was just what she needed. She wished the situation with Germaine had not happened as it did. She had been feeling overwhelmed for a while but did not mean for it to come out that way. She wanted to call him but was not ready just yet. She wanted to take this all in for a little bit longer.

She loved Germaine and the kids and couldn't understand why she was so emotional about his family. She knew they had gotten over the fact that she was a single mother, and they never cared about her skin color. She knows that his mom loves her like a daughter. She just couldn't shake these feelings. She walked into the bathroom and picked up the stick that she left on the counter last night. She had completely forgotten that she had taken a pregnancy test. She was so drained from everything that happened that it completely slipped her mind.

Jennifer plopped down on the toilet in disbelief as she read the plus sign on the test. She picked up the box again to read what the plus sign meant even though she already knew. She hoped it would mean something different this time, but of course, it did not. She was pregnant. How was that possible? She had her tubes tied after she had Ben, so it did not make sense. She raced to the dining room table and grabbed her cell phone. She quickly dialed her gynecologist's phone number but received the voice mail. She forgot it was the weekend; the office wasn't open.

"Dang! I need to know how far along I am." She said aloud still in disbelief. She went ahead and dialed her house number. Germaine picked up on the first ring.

"Hello."

"Hey, Maine," She said feeling really guilty at the sound of his voice.

"Hey babe; you okay?" He said, openly concerned.

"Yeah, I'm okay. Look, Maine, I'm sorry how I reacted the other day. I was wrong, and I should have stayed to talk it out, but I really did need this time to myself." Jennifer stated with a sigh of relief.

"I wish we could have talked about it, but I understand that you need your space, it's fine. Just come home when you are ready." Germaine could not believe he was saying this as he wanted his wife home now.

"Thank you, sweetie; I will be home tomorrow. Germaine, I love you, and thank you so much for understanding." She was practically smiling. She was so blessed to have such a good husband.

"It's no problem, babe. I love you too. You are my rib! You know that. I must make sure you are taken care of. I will see you tomorrow. Be careful."

Jennifer hung up with Germaine feeling a lot better. Now if she could just figure out what is going on with this pregnancy test? She pulled out her laptop and booked the first flight out of Malibu. She had some time before her flight, so she lay down to take a nap and enjoy the last bit of peace she was going to have for a while. Just when she started into the deep sleep, she rushed to the bathroom to throw up. She had been doing that all night long.

'I guess this is morning sickness,' she thought. 'Yuck! I can't stand throwing up. It takes forever to get the taste to go away.'

Jennifer ordered room service and could barely wait for it to come. She was starving. She tipped the man and ran to the food. Hmmm, fruit pizza, and yogurt. Now if the baby didn't like this, then there was going to be a big problem. This was her favorite breakfast.

She gulped the food down so fast she hardly felt herself take a breath. Next, she followed it down with the entire glass of orange juice. She tried lying down again. This time it worked like a charm. She was out like a light.

7.

JUANITA

Juanita pulled her Cadillac sedan into one of their three-car garages. She had just come from church and was feeling a little tired. She and the kids went into the house, and she headed to the kitchen as part of her normal Sunday routine. Every Sunday, after church, she would cook breakfast and dinner. She started to pull the pots and pans out from the cabinets extremely loud to awaken Chris. Juanita stopped and set everything down on the counter. She had to collect herself. This was stupid. She had not spoken to Chris since Thanksgiving night, and it completely contradicted the sermon from church this morning. 'Don't take things for granted. Don't allow your feelings to get in the way of an important relationship. Always be sure that you tell your loved ones that you love them and how important they are to you because none of us know when the end will come.' The Pastor had said during the service. 'I'm going to be the bigger person and just squash this because it is useless.' She walked up the stairs and into their bedroom.

She saw Chris in the shower and came up behind him as he was getting out. She wrapped her arms around his waist.

"Stop Nita; what are you doing?" Chris said, aggravated, removing her arms.

"Just trying to get a hug," Juanita said in a childish voice. "Chris, I'm sorry for the way I acted on Thursday. It wasn't the right time to discuss that. I'm not saying I don't feel that way, but I could have handled it better. Do you forgive me?" She said, giving her best puppy dog face.

Chris pulled his wife close to him and hugged her tight. He could never stay mad at her. "I forgive you, baby. I think we need to talk about it. This is not the first time we have fought over this. Do you really think I drink too much?"

"Yes, I do. Case in point, I saw you passed out in the bed the night of the fight with the Patron in hand. You had already had Hennessy and no telling what else."

Juanita walked over and sat on their bed as she watched Chris put on his boxers.

"The last thing I want to do is upset you. I will slow down on the alcohol babe."

"I really appreciate it."

"Come on, baby. Let's go get something to eat. I'm starving."

"Oh! I was just about to cook breakfast..."

"Yeah, I know, but that's the point. Let's do something different. How about I take you to Copeland's? They have a delicious brunch menu!" Chris was getting excited at the thought of his favorite restaurant. He continued putting on his clothes.

"Okay, I'm down with that!" Juanita said as she headed to her closet to find something to change into.

Juanita was overjoyed. She had made up with her husband, and they were going to their favorite restaurant. She made a smart decision to discuss this with her husband; she felt good about it.

Chris' cell phone rang while they were eating. He was a little surprised to see that his brother was calling on a Sunday.

"Hey, bro what's up?" Chris said, stuffing fried fish into his mouth.

"Hey Chris, I..." Anthony started to cry again.

"Ant. Hey man. What's wrong?" Chris said, starting to get anxious.

"Um, it's Danielle," Anthony stated through his tears; "She was in a car accident on Friday morning. She's in critical condition."

"What?!" Chris exclaimed in disbelief at the news and astonishment that he was just now calling him. "What hospital are you guys at?" Chris asked while waving down the waitress.

"She's at Grady Memorial Hospital. Mom is on her way here to get Bradley for me. I haven't been home yet." Anthony said, wiping his tears.

"I'm sorry to hear that man. We are at a Copeland's so as soon as I can pay, we will be on our way. What's the room number?"

"It's room 215."

"Okay, we're on our way."

"Thanks for coming, man. I really didn't want to bother you." Anthony said, relieved.

Juanita was staring at Chris with a look of concern, "What's going on?"

"Danielle was in a car accident on Friday, and she is in critical condition. I told him we would come down to the hospital. He said Mom is on her way down there to get Bradley for him. I just don't understand why he waited so long to contact us." Chris said still in disbelief.

"Oh, my goodness," Juanita gasped, shaking her head,

"We have to go. I can't believe this. We just saw them." This brought back to her remembrance what service was about today. 'Oh Lord, please do not tell me she is going   to die.'

8.

ANTHONY

Anthony paced the room back and forth, stopping every couple of seconds to look at his wife in the hospital bed. He could not believe this was happening. He could not stop thinking about what the policeman said to him about the accident. Why would someone intentionally try to hurt Danielle? He sat down in the chair next to her bed, held her hand, and cried.

Chris and Juanita walked into the room. Chris walked over to Anthony and put his hand on his shoulder to console him. Anthony looked up, stood, and hugged his brother. He was relieved that he was there. Juanita walked over and hugged Anthony as well. Chris asked Anthony the burning question, "What happened?" Chris and Juanita both found chairs and say, giving Anthony their undivided attention.

Anthony wiped his face and tried to collect himself as he told his brother all he knew. "The police said that the accident must have been a hit and run. When they arrived at the scene, they saw her car pushed up onto the sidewalk wrapped around a tree. The entire driver's side was smashed in, but there weren't any other cars around. The weird thing about it is, the police said the way her SUV was hit it was as if someone had intentionally run into her. I just can't understand why someone would want to hurt her intentionally. I mean I know I have made some enemies over the years with my practice, but still, no one has ever tried to hurt my family or me or even threatened us," Anthony said trying to fight back more tears while holding Danielle's hand. "The doctors are still running tests, so they won't know for sure until Monday if she has any brain damage. Danielle has been unconscious ever since they found her. She had four broken ribs, and her left lung was collapsed. They have not seen any brain activity yet, so they believe she may have some fluid that is causing her head to swell. It just does not look good."

Chris walked over to Anthony and hugged him again. He had never seen his brother cry before except when dad died. He was crushed. He did not know what to say to him to console him. He wanted to tell him everything would be alright, but he didn't believe it himself after listening to his brother run down the laundry list of things wrong with Danielle.

Just then, Danita walked in. Her face said it all; she already knew everything. She went around and hugged everyone. She informed Anthony that she would take Bradley home with her and to keep her updated. He told her he would as he gave her one last hug. Danita stopped before leaving the room. She made her way over to the hospital bed; put her hand on Danielle's forehead, and said a prayer. She went ahead and took Chris and Juanita's boys as well.

Anthony was relieved his mom laid hands on Danielle even though he did not believe in prayer and God. He knew his mom did, and she was the only one that could help Danielle right now. Ever since his father died of a heart attack five years ago, he has been upset with God believing that He did not exist. 'If He exists, then why didn't dad recover from his heart attack like we prayed for?' He recalled asking his mom. The only thing she could say was that 'some things just don't have an explanation.' That just didn't make sense.

Chris and Juanita stayed at the hospital with Anthony that night; helping him in any way they could so he could try to get some rest. But it was obvious he couldn't sleep; he was a wreck. During the night, the nurses would come in and check on Danielle; changing catheters, fluids, and checking her vital signs. Juanita was sleep when Anthony asked Chris to talk with him outside of the room. Chris followed his brother as directed.

"Hey man, I can't get this out of my head so I will just go ahead and say it. I think her accident was my fault." Anthony managed to get out teary-eyed.

"What do you mean? It was an accident. How could it have been your fault?" Chris said, confused.

"Danielle and I got into an argument Thanksgiving night. I grabbed her and yelled at her. I know I shouldn't have, but I was upset. That was the last time we spoke to each other. I believe she was probably still upset and wasn't paying attention to where she was going or something." Anthony started rubbing his temples as if that would help it all to make sense.

"Ant, man; I don't think you hear what you are saying. Danielle is one of the only people I know that could drive in any type of anything. She is an excellent driver. It's something else going on, but I don't know what it is. You can't blame yourself though, Ant. What were you fighting about? I mean if you don't want to tell me, I understand." Chris put his hand on his brother's shoulder, trying to console him.

"We had just got home and gotten settled. Bradley couldn't sleep so Dee went to put him back to bed when the phone rang. I answered it, of course. It was a dude calling for Dee. He acted like he could care less that I was her husband; almost like I was just her roommate. So, I went and got her, and that's what started the argument. She told me he was a co-worker and she didn't know how he got our number."

"Did you listen to their conversation?"

"No. I trust her. I just didn't appreciate that dude calling."

"Oh, okay. So, why is this bothering you?"

"Because I broke my rule," Anthony said, getting heated; "We are never supposed to go to bed angry at each other. We are always supposed to talk it out, and I didn't do that. Now, I may never get the chance to apologize."

"Man, I'm pretty sure that Dee knows you are sorry."

They both walked back into the room. Chris sat next to Juanita and laid his head back, trying to get a little comfortable to go to sleep. Anthony slid in the bed with Danielle and fell right to sleep.

Later that morning, the doctor came in to speak to Anthony. Dr. Vargas explained to him that the radiology team would come in soon to get Danielle to take her for CAT scans and MRI to find out how much brain activity she is having. He stated that at that point, they would go over the results with the neurologist and determine her prognosis. Anthony shook his head in agreement and understanding. The nurse came in and checked Danielle's vitals once more, and then Anthony laid back down next to his wife.

While Anthony slept, Chris pulled Juanita out of the room to tell her about the conversation he and Anthony had the night before. Juanita was flabbergasted. She had never spoken to Danielle about there being anyone else, possibly bothering her or calling the house. Juanita tried to assure Chris that the phone call probably didn't mean anything, especially anything that was pertinent to the current situation. Chris nodded his head in agreement but was still skeptical. Juanita told him that she would stay the day with them in the hospital but would have to leave to get the boys from his mom. He told her he understood; he went with her to the cafeteria to get breakfast and some coffee for Anthony. As they got on the elevator, Chris just could not shake the uneasy feeling he was having about that phone call. He would do a little research of his own.

9.

MARIE

Marie woke up still unable to believe what she saw on the videotape. How could her husband have gotten mixed up in some crazy stuff like this? And, how did she not know about it? She didn't realize how oblivious she had been. She was just the trusting, credulous wife that never asked any questions or never once investigated their finances. She let Marc handle everything, and the only thing she had to do was take care of the kids.

She was so lost in her thoughts that she did not hear the phone ringing, "Hello." Marie had to run to the phone.

"Hello. Is this Marie Smith?"

"Yes, how can I help you?" Marie did not recognize this woman's voice.

The woman cleared her throat, "You don't know me, but my name is Gwendolyn Smith. I knew your husband, Marc. I..." She hesitated. "I really think that we should meet. I have something that I believe you want to see regarding Marc." Gwendolyn's voice was soft-spoken but assertive.

"What exactly is this about Gwendolyn? I really don't have time for games." Marie felt herself becoming agitated.

"Really, I believe you will want to meet with me. I'm at work today and would love to meet with you. You will want to hear what I have to say. Plus, I have several things you need to see regarding Marc. Can you please meet me at the Federal Atlantic Bank downtown?" Gwendolyn's voice was a little sterner this time.

"Fine, what time?" Her curiosity was getting the best of her by this point. She genuinely wanted to know what this woman was talking about.

"Are you able to meet me around 1 p.m.?" Gwendolyn checked her calendar to see what time she would be available.

"That's fine. See you then." Marie's voice was dry.

She had to admit that she was very anxious about this meeting with Gwendolyn; thinking about what information she could provide. Marie woke the boys; made sure they got dressed and got them off to school. She called her job to let them know that she would not be into work today. She did one last check in her rearview mirror to ensure her makeup was intact as she headed downtown to the Federal Atlantic Bank to meet with Gwendolyn.

When she arrived, she was surprised at how quickly she was able to find parking.

She whipped her Volkswagen station wagon into the space, grabbed the parking slip, and headed to the elevator. When Marie walked inside the bank, she was amazed. She had never been inside this certain bank before, but it was a sight to see. The artistry work was just breathtaking. From the paintings to the statues, she was just in complete awe. She went to the line and asked one of the tellers to direct her to Gwendolyn Smith. The teller informed her that Gwen was in a meeting but to sign in on the sign-in sheet and have a seat. She would let her know that she was waiting. Marie did as she was told. It was almost cliché. Why be different now? Why change now, Marie? She smirked at herself that she would think of this now.

The same teller walked towards her and directed her to follow her. Marie did as she was directed. She thanked the teller for the assistance and introduced herself to Gwendolyn. She was a little jealous seeing this woman in person now. She was gorgeous but with a familiar face. Marie did not have low self-esteem. She knew she was beautiful, but after seeing this woman, she felt a little self-conscious.

Gwendolyn had flawless skin. She looked to be 5'7 easily, but with the three-inch heels she was wearing, she looked like a giant towering over her. She had a long flowing ponytail which she was quite confident was a weave. She had on a two-piece pin-stripe skirt suit with a ruffle blouse. She could not take her eyes from her.

Gwendolyn jumped right into the matter at hand, "Thank you, Mrs. Smith, for meeting with me. I know my phone call this morning must have seemed very abrupt. I apologize for that." She said as she collected some items from a locked drawer in her desk.

"Yeah, I have to admit I did think you were a little crazy," Marie stated as she shifted herself in the chair.

Gwendolyn handed Marie a stack of papers. Marie took them and started to sift through them. She didn't understand what she was looking at.

"Mrs. Smith, Marc was an over the road truck driver as I know you are aware. We met about a year ago when I was in South Carolina. I worked at a bank there, and he came in to withdraw money. We hit it off immediately. He took me to dinner that night, and we spoke quite often after that." Gwendolyn paused to give Marie time to take it all in. "Are you okay? Can I continue?" She asked.

"Yes," was all Marie could say.

"So, about four months into the relationship, Marc brought up the subject of moving in together. He did explain that because he was a trucker, he would not be home often, but he wanted us to be a family as I already had a one-year-old son. I'm pretty sure you could imagine my excitement, so I said yes. We moved in together that following month and were married in September of last year."

Gwendolyn stopped and took a deep breath, "I was so happy. Marc never showed any signs or gave me any indication that he was already married or even reason to suspect there was anyone else but me. I heard about a truck driving accident on the news six months ago, and when I reached out to the police, they had no idea who I was or what I was talking about. I had been going back and forth with the police and the coroner because, of course, they would not release the body to me. One day my sister showed me Marc's obituary. The same obituary stated that he was married and listed your name and your children. I was in disbelief. The papers I handed to you are our marriage certificate, bank statements, medical insurance policy, and etcetera."

Tears were rolling down Gwendolyn's face by now. Marie did not know what to think. She was angry, disappointed, and felt betrayed. Why did her husband do this to her, to their family, and Gwen? She was truly hurt. After the video she found, she knew what Gwendolyn was saying was true.

"Ms. Smith…" Marie started.

"Please, call me Gwen," she interrupted.

"Alright, Gwen, I don't want you to take what I am going to say the wrong way. I was married to my husband for a very long time. I loved my husband, and I believe that he loved me as well. It is a little difficult to internalize this information. You want me to believe that my husband married you and was a father to your son even though he was married to me?" Marie glared at Gwen.

"Marie, the proof is there in the paperwork I handed you. Also," Gwen picked up a photo off her desk and handed it to her, "We had this taken last Christmas Eve." It was a portrait of Marc, Gwen, and her son in front of a Christmas tree.

Marie could feel the sting of the tears burning behind her eyes. She could not believe what she was seeing and hearing. This was beyond anything she could ever imagine. She thought her husband was perfect. She thought their life was perfect. She thought they had the perfect family. People would genuinely tell her that she had the perfect family. She just kept shaking her head as if this would cause her to wake up from this nightmare.

"Marie, I can honestly say I know how you feel. I felt the same way when I read the obituary. I felt betrayed, hurt, dismayed. The list goes on." Gwen grabbed a tissue from her desk and dabbed her eyes. She handed a tissue to Marie as well.

Gwen reached for Marie's hand, "I'm so sorry for our loss. I'm pretty sure he meant just as much to you as he did to me. I'm not telling you about this to hurt you. I just felt like you should know."

Marie rubbed Gwen's hand and informed her that she understood her reasoning. This was a lot to take in. She apologized to her for the accusation and decided it was time to leave.

10.

DANITA

Danita rolled out of bed after the alarm went off for the third time. She sat on the edge of the bed and gathered her thoughts. She knelt next to the bed and said another prayer for Danielle and each member of her family. Danita got up, took a shower, and headed downstairs to fix her grandbabies some breakfast. It was 8:30 a.m. She had not gotten up this early in a long time. She had gotten Bradley from Anthony yesterday so he could concentrate on Danielle. Juanita decided to let their boys stay the night as well to allow Chris to stay with Anthony, and she needed to go to work. She did not want to dwell on the incident with Danielle, but she could not get over it. She knew that God answered prayers; she just has to keep her trust and faith that He will bring her out of this.

The kids were already up as she could hear them in their rooms playing. She continued downstairs to the kitchen to prepare breakfast. She was almost finished with the eggs when her phone rang.

"Hello," she answered a little exasperated.

"Hey, Ma! What are you doing?" Germaine asked very enthusiastic this morning.

"Hey sweetie, I'm cooking breakfast for the kids. What are you doing?" Danita asked as she set the table.

"What kids?"

Danita paused and realized that she had not told him about Danielle's accident.

"Maine, have you spoken to Anthony?" She asked, trying to figure out how to tell him.

"Um, no, I haven't spoken to him since I think…Thanksgiving? Why? What's up?"

"Germaine, Anthony is at Grady. Danielle was in a car accident on Friday morning. She is in critical condition. I have Bradley. Chris and Juanita went to the hospital yesterday, so I have John and Justin as well. I'm so sorry I'm just now telling you. I thought that when Chris came to the hospital, well, I assumed Anthony had called you too. Oh, my goodness! I wonder if he called Marie." Danita said as she sat down.

Germaine was taken aback; he didn't know what to say. "Ma, what's the phone number to the hospital? And, what room is she in?" He said as he was trying to find a pen and paper.

Danita gave him the hospital phone number and room information. She apologized again for not telling him sooner as they hung up.

Danita took in a deep breath and called Marie. She almost breathed a sigh of relief when she got her voice mail. She left a very vague message on the machine to give her a quick call. She wondered where Marie was though. She was normally at work and answered her calls immediately. Danita shrugged it off thinking maybe she had some errands to run.

She told the kids to wash their hands and called them down to eat breakfast. She loved to cook. It seemed to take her mind off things. She made scrambled eggs, cheese grits, salmon croquettes, homemade buttermilk biscuits, and freshly squeezed orange juice. The kids all piled at the table and wolfed down the food like they had not eaten in years.

Danita missed spending time with her grandbabies. She had not seen them in a while well except for Thanksgiving. It was time for them to spend some time with their Nana. Maybe this would be the time for her to get all her grandkids?

After stuffing their faces and only leaving a small number of leftovers; she had the kids work together to do the dishes. She then instructed them to wash up and put on clothes. She warmed up her Suburban and decided she would take them to Jump Zone or Chuck-E-Cheese. About forty-five minutes later, everyone was ready to go. They all piled into the SUV and Danita pulled out of the garage. She had to slam on brakes to avoid hitting the vehicle pulling up in the driveway. When she looked closer, she realized it was Marie. She put the SUV in park and got out.

"Marie, what are you doing here? Did you get my message?"

Marie didn't say a word. She just walked over to her mother and wrapped her arms around her. She needed someone to hold her right now, and there was no better person to do that than her mom. Danita hugged her back no questions asked. Danita told the kids to get out of the car so she could go in and talk to Marie. They did as they were told but let her know through all the moans and groans that they were not happy about it. Danita ignored it, this time only since she had something more important to handle. Danita walked with Marie back into the house and into the living room as all the kids went upstairs.

"Marie baby, what's wrong?" Danita said, getting even more concerned.

"Mom; I just came from the bank, and I can't believe what I found out," Marie managed to get out through her sobs. "I received a call from a woman that works at a bank downtown this morning. She called me to tell me that she knew Marc and she wanted to discuss his death with me."

Marie got up and grabbed a napkin from the table to wipe her nose; she continued, "Of course, I was curious about what she had to say, so I went down there. The weird thing is I recently found a VCR tape in a box in Marc's closet and then to get a call from her. Mom, the tape was of Marc spending Christmas day with a woman and her son. The tape was not dated, so I didn't know when it was, but the woman from the video was the same woman I met with."

Danita didn't know what to say. She just sat there holding Marie's hand for support.

"I met with this woman, Gwendolyn. I mean Gwen, this morning after I dropped off the boys at school. We talked for well over two hours about how she came to know Marc, and she showed me all sorts of information. Mom, she is his wife. The boy in the video is her son, and Marc adopted him."

"What?!" Danita asked in shock. "Is she serious?" She could not believe what she was hearing.

"Yes Mom, she was serious, and I believe her. I can't believe all this was going on and I didn't even know about it. She loved him. You could see it in her eyes when she talked about him. I was so disgusted and hurt. You were the first person I could think of to tell. Mom, I need your advice. What do I do? I'm so confused. I want to hurt someone right now." Marie was crying uncontrollably by this time.

She consoled her the best way she knew how. Danita just held Marie and let her cry. She fell asleep on Danita's lap. Danita laid her down on the couch and put a blanket over her. She went upstairs to check on the kids in the playroom, and they were sleeping as well. Danita went to her room and started today's journal entry. She fell asleep before she made it to the end of the page.

11.

GERMAINE

Germaine sat at his desk, still dumbfounded from what his mom had just informed him. He knew he needed to call his brother so he could be there for him in his time of need. He was trying not to feel selfish and think about himself, but he could not help but wonder why Anthony did not call him and tell him; especially if he called Chris. Germaine's receptionist interrupted his thoughts when she came to let him know that his last patient had left. He thanked her and told her she could wrap up and leave for the day. He knew he needed to take himself out of the equation and just think about Anthony and Danielle.

Germaine called Anthony's cell, but he received the voice mail, so he left a message, 'Hey man it's Maine. Mom just told me about Danielle. I'm heartbroken. Call me; I want to talk to you. I will be at the hospital a little later. I have to finish closing up here.'

Germaine got up to put on his coat when his cell rang. "Hello, Ant?" He answered with a little bit of desperation and anxiousness.

"No, sweetie, it's me, Jennifer."

"Oh, hey, baby. How are you doing?" Germaine stated, trying to get his composure back.

"I'm good. You? You sound a little antsy."

"No, I'm good. I was waiting for a call from Anthony. I thought you were him calling me back. What's up?" He said as he turned off the lights in his office and walked towards the door to lock up.

"Nothing, I wanted to know what your plans were today. I'm trying to plan a quiet night for us tonight and wanted to know what time you would be home." Jennifer was very exuberant about this dinner. She had been home for almost twenty-four hours and needed to tell Germaine the news.

"Uh well, baby. I'm actually heading over to Grady Hospital now to meet up with Anthony. What time were you planning to have dinner?"

"Well, maybe about 6:30 or 7. Why are you meeting Anthony at the hospital?" Jennifer was curious at this point.

"Danielle is in the hospital, and I'm going over there," Germaine said as he walked to his car in the parking garage.

Jennifer gasped, "Elle is in the hospital? What happened?" She shook her head in incredulity.

"I'm not sure of the details, but when I talked to Ma, she said she had been in a car accident. Apparently, this happened on Friday."

"I wanna come too. Can you come get me, or I can meet you somewhere? Oh wait, what am I going to do with Tyrone and Ben?"

"I can call Ma to see if she would mind if you dropped them off for a little while." Germaine thought since she was watching everyone else's kids.

"So, you want me to drop the kids off on the way to meet you? How do you want to handle that?" Jennifer was starting to get aggravated because she did not want to do all this driving.

"I tell you what; I will call Ma and see if she would mind first. If she says it's okay, then I will head your way, and we can go together."

"Okay, that's fine; just let me know. I love you," Jennifer said relieved.

"I love you too. I will call you back after I talk to Ma."

"Okay baby." Jennifer headed upstairs and started packing the boys an overnight bag just in case.

Twenty minutes had passed, and he was still waiting for his mom to call him back; which was a little unusual. He was sitting at the red light when his cell phone rang.

"Hello," he answered without even looking at the caller id. He was more anxious this time than before.

"Hey man, what's up?" Anthony said fatigued.

"Not much is up with me; what's up with you? How's Danielle doing?" Germaine asked anxiously.

Anthony started to cry again, "The doctor said she is coming around. They ran some tests this morning, and we waited all day for the specialist to become available so they could go over the results. Her brain is showing signs of activity, which is what they were nervous about initially. She's not completely out of the woods, but they are assuring me that this is a good sign. She looks so vulnerable. It hurts knowing that there's nothing I can do."

Now Germaine felt helpless, "Hey man; all you can do is pray for her. I'm pretty sure Ma laid hands on her. You just have to keep praying, trusting, and believing that God will pull her through this."

"See, for that reason right there, is why I didn't call you when it happened! Because I knew you were going to start your 'Holier than thou' speech. I have not spoken to God since dad died, and I don't plan to either. I didn't want to get a lecture. I just want her to be better." Anthony said, heated at his brother and ready to hang up on him.

"I'm not trying to lecture you, Ant. I'm letting you know what is going to make the difference. I was upset that dad died too, but you cannot blame God. I'm telling you that you are the one that is going to make a difference in Danielle's healing. As soon as you get over your anger and come back to God and trust and believe in Him; He will pull her through in a miraculous way." Germaine was trying not to let his little brother upset him but wanted him to understand.

"Yeah whatever you say, man. Look I gotta go. I'll talk to you later." Anthony hung up without waiting for Germaine's response.

Germaine never could understand why he and his brother were like oil and water ever since their dad died; they used to be so close. It bothered him. He knows that his father would not be happy about it. Anthony could be so immature sometimes.

Germaine was so caught up in his thoughts that it took a minute for him to realize his cell was ringing. "Hello," Germaine had a slight attitude but was hoping that Anthony had come to his senses and called back to apologize.

"Hey, pumpkin. You sound like you are ready to fight. You must have spoken to Anthony?" Danita could always tell when Germaine has gotten into it with Anthony. He always allowed that boy to get under his skin.

"Oh, hi Ma," Germaine was a little disappointed. He really wanted that apology.

"I was calling you back. I must have dozed off. I didn't even hear the phone ring. What was it that you needed pumpkin?"

"Well, I wanted to see if you would keep the boys for us so we could go to the hospital, but after speaking with Anthony, I don't think we should go down there," Germaine stated sulking and still irritated with his brother.

Danita tried to sound as sincere as she could, "Maine, honey, it's up to you whether you go down there or not. Don't let Anthony determine what you do. You know I have no problem watching my grandbabies. You and that wife of yours need some time alone anyway." Danita chuckled.

"Thanks, Mom. What do you mean we need some time alone? Why would you think that?" Germaine asked defensively as if she knew they were having problems.

"Boy! You are married with children. All parents need a break from time to time. Why do you think we left you all with your grandparents twice a month?" She chuckled again.

"Huh? Really? Granddaddy told us it was because you were on business trips. I always wondered why you couldn't take us." Germaine was surprised that his mom never shared this with him before.

"Yeah, they were business trips, alright. Your daddy took care of a lot of business while we were gone." Danita was shaking her head in reminiscence of the hotel stays. She chuckled again.

"Okay, okay, Mom. I really don't want that thought in my head, okay. I get the point. I appreciate you watching the kids for us. I will let Jennifer know."

"No, don't call her. I want to talk to her. I feel like we don't talk that often. I want to change that. I am close to all my daughters (in law) except her. I feel like she has a wall up for some reason. I'm not that far away from your house. I can stop by there and get the boys." Danita was already figuring out a different route to go to get to Germaine's house.

"Uh, that's fine. Just be sure you call her before you get there. I should be home soon. Thanks again,

Mom!" He felt like one huge weight had been lifted now he just needed to work on the other one.

12.

JENNIFER

Jennifer lay on the couch while she waited for Germaine to get home. She was winded and tired from running around trying to get the kids' clothes together for Danita; who had just left from picking the kids up. Jennifer hoped she did not forget anything. She felt terrible for Anthony and Danielle's situation but could not help but feel a little guilty as she did see this as an opportunity for her and Germaine to be alone. She went to the doctor this morning, and her gynecologist performed an ultrasound. It was confirmed she was ten weeks along. Jennifer was a little nervous because they had not discussed having more kids, so she had no idea how Germaine would react. She wasn't sure how she felt about it. She had to admit that after seeing the baby on the sonogram, it brought all those feelings back of being overjoyed and in love all over again. Just as she started to doze off, she heard the garage door open.

She grabbed her purse, walked over to the mudroom, put on her heels, and headed out the door.

"Hey honey," Jennifer said as Germaine walked towards her giving her a quick peck on the lips.

"Hey, baby. You can go ahead and get in. I have to use the restroom really quickly," Germaine said as he walked into the house.

Jennifer did as she was instructed and got settled into the passenger side of their BMW SUV. She hadn't realized that she dozed off until she heard her husband yelling at the car in front of them while honking his horn because they cut him off. She woke up startled. "You okay?" She asked Germaine sarcastically knowing that he was not.

"Of course, I am. At least I was until that idiot cut me off. I didn't mean to wake you. You were sleeping like a baby; so beautiful." Germaine put his hand on Jennifer's leg.

"Yeah, I must have been more tired than I thought. I didn't even realize I dozed off. Dang, I don't even remember pulling out of the garage." Jennifer said as she laughed at herself. Germaine returned the laugh as well because he knew she was right. She was out before they left the house. "I guess the question is, are you okay? You've been very tired lately?"

"Can you tell me what happened with Danielle?" Jennifer asked, attempting to pivot by holding off that conversation until later.

"I don't know. Mom just said she was in a car accident. I didn't get too many details out of Ant as far as what took place. He did say that the doctors were running a lot of tests. They did notice brain activity, which is good as they were concerned initially, but she is still unconscious. You know he and I got into it again so I wasn't even sure that I should go down there, but he needs his family right now." Germaine was hurt by the conversation he had with his brother.

"You're right. I know you guys have your differences, but he needs any and all the support he can get right now." Jennifer grabbed Germaine's hand and intertwined their fingers. "Um, what were your plans for dinner? Did you want to pick up something at the hospital or go out to eat?" Jennifer was hungry again but thanked God she had not experienced a lot of 'morning sickness,' since the other day.

"You know what? That's a good question. I hadn't even thought about that, but I am hungry. Maybe we should go out to eat since we don't have the kids tonight? Are you hungry?" Germaine just realized that he didn't eat lunch. He missed having Jennifer at the office. She always made sure he ate.

"I'm definitely hungry. Going out to eat sounds like a great idea! Since we are going to Grady, we could probably hit up one of the restaurants within the vicinity?" Jennifer could feel herself getting excited.

"That's a great idea! You think about where you want to go when we leave the hospital, okay." Germaine said as he gently caressed Jennifer's cheek.

"You already know if we are going to Atlanta, where I want to go, McCormick & Schmick's; my favorite restaurant." Jennifer was clapping and hopping in her seat like a child in Toys'R'Us.

Germaine started shaking his head but had to laugh at his wife. It never fails, when they are in this area that is the only restaurant she wants to go to. One day he was going to change her mind. "Okay, I won't argue with that today, but we will have to try something different at some point." Germaine kissed the back of Jennifer's hand, still laughing at her reaction.

"Okay, that's a deal. The next time we go downtown, we will try somewhere else."

They pulled up to the hospital and Germaine drove around to find somewhere to park. He could not stand going to Grady because it was always packed, but he did have to admit they were an excellent trauma hospital.

13.

MIKE

Anthony paced Danielle's room. It did not seem to help calm him down, but he could not leave her side. He thought that if she could hear his voice, she would come out of it. The doctors said that she is stable, but they do not have realistic expectations that she will recover. They informed him this morning that they would have to wait and see. 'Wait and see! Wait and see! They are doctors! Why can't they tell me more than that?' Anthony was upset. He wanted answers, and he wanted his wife back. He wanted things back the way they were. Anthony sat in the chair next to the bed and held his wife's hand.

"God, I know I have not spoken to you in a while, well, since daddy died. I was and still am upset with you. I don't understand if you love us so much, why would you let my father die. We needed him here and still do. I used to be so close to you. I used to go to church and spend time with you. I want to change

Lord. I am coming to you today with a humble heart. Please heal Danielle. The doctors said there is nothing else they can do, but I know this is the time when you show up so everyone will give You the praise. I have nowhere else to turn because I know at this point, you are the only one that can heal her. Thank you for listening to me. I hope you don't hold a grudge as I have. I'm sorry for the way that I treated you. I promise if you heal her, I will ensure that we will start going to church and serving you, Lord. I want to have that relationship that we used to have. I want my wife back and the life that we had before all this happened. Please, I'm begging you. Jesus name. Amen."

Anthony opened his eyes and looked up at his wife. He loved her so much and just wanted her to get better. He didn't realize there was someone else in the room until the gentleman cleared his throat. Anthony wiped his eyes and introduced himself, "How you doing man? My name is Anthony. I'm Danielle's husband? Who are you?"

"I'm Mike," the gentleman said as he made his way over to Danielle's bed.

Anthony stared at the gentleman, confused. He was an older, clean cut, bald-headed man that was taller than him. He had to be 6'5 at least 230 pounds. The thing that bewildered Anthony was the scars on the man's face. It looked like he had been in an altercation or an accident himself.

"So, Mike, are you a nurse or something?" Anthony asked as this man grabbed his wife's hand.

"Naw man, I work with Danielle," Mike said as tears ran down his cheek while he held her hand close to his face.

Then Anthony thought about it; could this be the same dude that called their house the night before the accident. Anthony walked over to Mike and pushed him against the wall. He didn't care how big he was. "Why are you here? Are you the one that called my house Thursday night? Who are you?"

Mike blurted out, "I'm in love with Danielle. We've been dating for a while. She didn't show up for work and has not been answering her phone. I was getting concerned. One of our co-workers called me this morning and let me know she was here. I just wanted to see her. I can't believe this happened." He said as tears rolled down his face; "The people at the job are saying she is going to die. That can't be true."

Anthony could not believe what he was hearing. Has this man lost his mind? Maybe he was telling the truth. He couldn't be. Danielle would never do anything like that. Anthony lost it. He punched Mike in the face like it was a punching bag. He took out all his frustrations and anger on him. Mike fell to the floor, and Anthony kicked him over and over landing kicks to his ribs, stomach, and groin.

Germaine walked into Danielle's room and saw his brother. He pulled him off the gentleman and took him out of the room. Germaine slammed Anthony against the wall.

"Man, what are you doing? Have you lost your mind?" Germaine said, confused.

"Dude let me go! Let me go now, Maine!" Anthony said, trying to get free from his brother, but somehow, Germaine's grip was stronger.

"No! Not until you tell me what is going on." Germaine was steadfast. He was not moving, and Anthony would stay hemmed up against the wall for as long as it took.

Anthony took a deep breath and explained to Maine what Mike told him. Germaine calmly let Anthony go, "I'll handle this." He went into the hospital room with Mike, closed the door behind him, and locked it.

Mike was clutching Danielle's hand and still sobbing when Germaine walked in the room.

"Are you here to fight me too? I'm not leaving her side," Mike mumbled with his head down.

"No, I'm not going to hit you, but I do want to understand what is going on? My brother is not in a rational state of mind right now. You do realize that you told him that you are in love with his wife? I mean you understand why he lost it, right?" Germaine said as he sat down on the other side of Danielle to face Mike.

"Yea, I understand. I know he's upset and it's probably a shock to him. Elle said she would tell him about us, but I guess she didn't get around to it. I couldn't stay away when I found out what happened," Mike stated as he laid his head on Danielle's forearm.

Germaine looked at him, bewildered, "What do you mean; you love her? Are you saying that she feels the same way about you?"

"Of course; you think I would risk all of this coming down here if she didn't feel the same way about me!"

"How long has this been going on?" Germaine asked determined to get to the bottom of this.

"About six months," Mike said as he continued to hold his head down in shame knowing he was lying about their relationship.

"Was this a physical relationship or just emotional? I mean…"

"I know what you are trying to ask. It was both. She is everything to me; I would do anything for her."

"Okay, it's time for you to leave," Germaine said as he walked around the bed to escort Mike out.

Just then, Danielle let out a moan and fluttered her eyes. Germaine looked over at her and ran to get Anthony. Anthony ran to Danielle, calling her name.

Danielle's eyes fluttered several times until she was able to get them open. She looked at Anthony and tried to speak. All she could get out were moans.

"Hey baby; don't try to speak," Anthony said as tears streamed down his face again. Germaine had come back with the nurse by this time.

The nurse checked her vitals, called for the doctor, and left the room. Danielle smiled at Anthony. She scanned the room seeing Germaine, Jennifer, and Mike. Her eyes locked with Mike's and she moaned louder, reached for Anthony, and started to cry.

Germaine pushed Mike out of the room and called for one of the nurses. He told them that he was not family and should not be allowed in the room. They called for security and escorted him out.

"You're in the hospital baby. You were in a car accident. You are okay now," he told her while squeezing her hand.

Danielle moaned more a little louder each time until she could get her words out. "What- is- he- doing- here?

"I asked him the same thing. I don't think this is the best time to talk about this."

"Anth-ony," Danielle struggled to get out. "I was co-min-g to ta-lk to you a-b-out him the day of the ac-cid-ent."

Anthony rubbed her head, "Baby, we can talk about this later. I just want to make sure you are okay." He kissed her on the forehead as the nurse and doctor came in.

Anthony let the doctor run his tests, and the nurse took Danielle's vitals again while he went out in the hallway to talk to Germaine.

"Where's that punk at?" He looked around and asked.

"He left. What's up?" Germaine looked concerned.

"Danielle said she was coming to talk to me about him the day of the accident. I told her we would discuss it later. Man, I'm so glad she pulled through. I prayed for her." Anthony said, trying to hold back tears.

Germaine hugged his brother, "I'm glad she pulled through too, bro. I'm so glad to hear you prayed for her. I know after dad died, you pulled away from

God. I hate that it took her accident to bring you back to Him, but I'm glad you did. As you can see, He brought her through."

"Yeah, I know He did. I told Him that only He was going to be able to heal her, especially since these doctors were playing the waiting game."

The brothers walked back into the hospital room right as the doctor and nurse were finishing up. Dr. Vargas pulled Anthony to the side to discuss her condition. Anthony pulled Germaine and Jennifer over as well. Dr. Vargas confirmed that he realized that her speech is slurred a little, which is normal with the amount of time she was in unconscious. Other than that, Dr. Vargas did not see any signs of any other type of trauma. Of course, he would have Radiology come to do more tests, but he felt optimistic. He mentioned that she might have some therapy to go through. Anthony was relieved.

"That's great news! Look, I'm going to go ahead and leave; unless you need me for anything else." Germaine said as he gave his brother a fist bump.

"No, man; you're good. Thanks for sticking it out with me. Look, I'm sorry for jumping down your throat earlier. I was just stressed. I know what you were telling me was what I needed to hear, but it wasn't what I wanted to hear." Anthony had a look of guilt and relief all at the same time.

"Man, you know I love you. I never want you to feel like I'm trying to tell you what to do, but I'm here for you." They hugged and then Anthony hugged Jennifer. Germaine and Jennifer walked over to Danielle, kissed her good-bye, thanked God for her recovery, and left.

Anthony caressed Danielle's head as they stared into each other's eyes.

"I- I want- to- talk- about- him," Danielle managed to get out through her slurred speech.

"No, we need to wait to discuss that. I need you completely healed and up and going. Don't worry; we will discuss it in detail," Anthony kissed her forehead, "Get some rest baby."

Danielle fell asleep. Anthony fixed up his pull-out chair next to the bed and fell asleep after watching his wife sleep soundly for about an hour. He felt a huge weight was lifted from his shoulders. He will call mom first thing in the morning to let her know the great news.

14.

TRYALS & TRYBULATIONS

Danita went around the house, making sure all the rooms were in order, and everything was tidied up. She went to the store earlier in the day and picked up quite a few groceries. She had started a tradition even before Paul passed that they would host Christmas. Their children and their families would come to their home on Christmas Eve to spend the night to be able to enjoy dinner, wrap presents, and wake up together. On Christmas, the children would be there to open their gifts. She normally makes breakfast on Christmas morning and has her daughters make the Christmas dinner. It was a two-day event that made them all so happy just enjoying the time and the family worship. 'It was 12:30 p.m. and they should be arriving at one but knowing them it will be closer to two.' Danita thought.

Danita pulled out the Christmas tree that Paul picked out so many years ago. She loved her Christmas tree. It was perfect, even if it was artificial. Each year Danita changed the theme of the tree. This year would be white and blue. The tree stood 10 feet tall, so without the kids' help, she was unable to get to the top. She decided to wait until they got there to assist in the decorating. She had managed to decorate part of the outside. She did her normal lighted garland around the windows and doors in the front of the home. She added wreaths with the snowy tips on the door, windows, and mailbox; but hired a company to complete the rest.

Danita started a pot of coffee and warmed milk for hot cocoa with marshmallows for the kids when she heard the doorbell ring. She dried her hands on her kitchen towel and tossed it on the counter.

She hurried to the door and opened it ready to greet her family. Danita stumbled back and froze. She couldn't believe her eyes. Was she dreaming? That was it! She was dreaming. It was a nightmare, and she would just wake herself up. But she wasn't dreaming. The brisk breeze of cold air was hitting her face ensuring her that this was real and no dream. Standing in front of her was Jeremy.

"Hi," he said with a nervous smile.

Danita did not respond. She couldn't. She blinked a few times and finally managed to get some words out. "What? What are you doing here?" Her voice trembling not from fear but because she could feel the anger, the rage, and confusion building up in her as she wanted to punch him in the face.

"I know I should not have just popped up, but you did not respond to my letter. We need to talk. It's been too long." Jeremy said, trying to plead his case exactly as he'd rehearsed it so many times before.

Danita shook her head as if that would make him go away. "I can't believe you have the nerve to show up at my door! Are you crazy?"

"No, I'm not. I really needed to see you so we can talk this out and I want to meet my son. I think I have been more than fair in allowing you time to heal. I want to meet my son, Danita."

"Heal. Heal! How dare you talk to me about healing?! I had to heal from my broken ribs! I had to HEAL from my broken jaw! I had to HEAL from all the things you did to me, not just physical but emotional. I had to HEAL and FORGIVE in order to be able to look at OUR son every day and not think of you! Don't you talk to me about healing!" Danita no longer cared about the cold breeze hitting her face. She was out on the porch with Jeremy at this point. She was so upset she was shaking.

Jeremy hung his head and changed his tone, "Danita, you are right. I have no right to ask anything of you. While I was in prison, I had time to think, nothing but time. I thought long and hard about what I did to you and how I ruined our relationship. I really did love you. I don't think I can apologize enough for what I did to you. I wrote you so many letters apologizing. At first, they were angry letters because I was so upset with you. I could not believe you would turn me in, let alone allow me to go to jail." Jeremy walked over to the swing and sat down. "What you don't understand or may not believe is that I was saved while I was in prison. My cellmate was a Christian, and he talked to me about Christ. I didn't want to listen to him at first, but I saw how much peace he had even in a terrible place like prison. The more we discussed Christ, the more I read the Bible, and went to Sunday service and was saved. That was fifteen years ago. I asked God to forgive me for what I did to you. The hardest part was forgiving myself. I know you probably don't believe me, but I have changed, and I hoped you would forgive me." Jeremy still had his head hung low, and tears began to fall from his eyes.

"I hope you didn't think it would be this easy. Yes, I forgave you but because I had to. I questioned my faith so many times while I was with you. I couldn't believe that I served a God that would allow those things to happen to me. Once I truly forgave you, I realized it was not God's doing that put me in that situation. I thank Him that I made it out. You need to understand that just because I forgave you, it does not mean I ever planned on you meeting my son. He had a father. One that took care of him and loved him like his own and was a provider. He was what he needed, and that is the only father he has ever known. I plan to keep it that way. I need you to get off my property before I call the police." Danita stood sternly in the doorway with arms folded.

Jeremy got up from the swing and walked over to Danita. "I'm truly sorry for everything I put you through. I can't imagine what that was like for you. I wish I had never done it. I wish I were the man that you see before you today. This is what you deserve, not what I was then. I'm not giving up. Understand that I heard you, but I still want to see my son." He walked off the porch and to his car and drove away.

Danita closed the door, walked to the hall half bathroom, looked in the mirror, and cried uncontrollably. She couldn't believe this just took place. She was so happy anticipating her children and a wonderful time but now this. Danita pulled herself together and wiped her face. She walked to the kitchen to pour herself some coffee. Instead of her usual creamer, she pulled a bottle of Jack Daniels down from the cabinet. She poured a small amount in it as it didn't take much for her. Danita started to drink the coffee when the doorbell rang.

She put the cup down on the counter, grabbed the baseball bat she had in the coat closet, and swung open the front door ready for a fight.

"Merry Christmas," Germaine yelled as she opened the door. "Ma, what's wrong?"

Danita put the bat down and hugged her son. She didn't want to let go.

"Mommy, what's wrong with Nana?" The boys asked. "Nothing, let's go inside so Nana and daddy can have some alone time."

"Mom, what's wrong?" Germaine asked, still holding her as tight as she was holding him.

"Nothing that I care to talk about right now; we'll talk later," Danita said as she pulled away and wiped the tears from her face.

"Mom, really?!" Germaine said, getting upset but trying not to disrespect her at the same time. "You are visibly, upset, and crying. You want me to just dismiss that?"

"Germaine, I said we would talk about it later. I can't right now." Danita walked back in the house and into the hall bathroom to clean up her face.

Germaine went into the kitchen to find Jennifer and the children at the eat-in kitchen table.

"Everything alright, babe?" Jennifer asked with some concern. The kids were pre-occupied with their handheld video games.

"Yeah, I guess. She won't tell me what's wrong." Germaine said irritated and confused.

Danita walked into the kitchen like nothing happened. She grabbed a hug from her grandchildren and then Jennifer. "Is anyone hungry?" Danita said, looking in the refrigerator.

"No, ma'am. "They all said in unison. "Okay, did you guys already put your things up?"

"Yes, ma'am," Jennifer responded. Germaine gave her a look in which she immediately knew what that meant. He does not like for her to lift the bags, etc.

"The boys took the bags to our room," Jennifer added before Germaine could even get started.

The doorbell rang. Danita went to the door. "Hey Mom, Merry Christmas!" Chris said, bombarding his mom for a hug. She hugged him back with a huge smile on her face, feeling relieved that it was not Jeremy coming back. She loved being with her family, especially now. This will for sure take her mind off things. "Merry Christmas sweetie!" She hugged Juanita and her grandchildren as they went into the house.

Chris headed upstairs with their luggage, dropped it in their respective rooms, and headed back downstairs. As he rounded the stairs, he saw his sister and brother come in the house. Chris immediately felt bad as he had not seen Anthony and Danielle since she was in the hospital, almost a month ago.

"Hey bro, what's up?" Anthony said, giving Chris a fist bump. Chris returned the gesture and gave a quick hug.

"I can't call it. Happy to see you guys. What's up with you?"

"A lot to talk about," Anthony whispered in his brother's ear. Chris nodded in understanding. He reached over and hugged Danielle who was walking with a cane but looked really well considering. He made sure to hug his sister as well who seemed like her mind was elsewhere.

Once in the house, everyone was busy discussing old times and getting settled. Danita had the men decorating the tree as she directed them each step of the way. The ladies were cooking the seafood dinner, and the kids were running around the house playing. After everyone had eaten, and the kids were put to bed, the adults got the presents together for the kids to begin wrapping.

They were all sitting on the couch, "I want to do something different this year." Danita said while wrapping a gift. "I want each one of us to tell something we are thankful for and/or what this year has meant to you. Jennifer, we'll start with you."

Jennifer was excited about being transparent as she felt they had a lot to be thankful and happy about. "Well, we are expecting. I'm seventeen weeks, and I am due in May!" She blew Germaine a kiss. "At first, I didn't know how to feel about it, but after I told Main, we are both excited and looking forward to it. I'm thankful for family."

"That's great, you guys!" Danita said overjoyed and genuinely excited for a new grandbaby. She jumped up and hugged both Germaine and Jennifer.

"Thanks, Ma! I didn't know how I felt about it initially, but I'm ecstatic. Jennifer's eating us out of house and home, but it's all good." Germaine couldn't stop laughing. Jennifer gave him the death stare that she had perfected for the kids.

"I want to say that this year has been a struggle for me, for us." Danielle struggled to get the words out tears in a steady stream down her face. "I put my family in danger without even realizing it. Constant flirting with my co-worker, Mike, we went to a work party and had too much to drink. When I woke up, he was on top of me. I don't even recall getting to that point." Danielle just kept shaking her head like that would make all of it go away.

"Then afterward, he would not leave me alone. He kept calling my cell and texting me, constantly trying to pull me in the storage closet at work or the bathroom if it was empty. I wanted to go to HR, but I was scared. I figured they would think I asked for it or I brought this on myself. All they would have to do is pull our text messages from when I was flirting. So, I didn't say anything. Never did I imagine this man would try to kill me."

Anthony walked over to Danielle, sat next to her on the couch, and rubbed her back to console her.

"I don't deserve this man right here. I screwed up! I...He forgave me. He nursed me back to health. He ensured that I got the best care. How do you even begin to thank someone for being selfless when they brought this on themselves? The doctors are telling me that I may never fully regain my ability to walk without this cane. But, to hear my husband tell me that he forgave me, so I need to forgive myself is beside me. He has breathed life back into me where I thought everything was hopeless. He prays for me. He prays with me. I hate that I did this thing to myself and my family, but I thank God that my husband has a relationship with the Lord again. It has changed our relationship. It has enhanced our marriage in ways I never thought was possible. I love you, babe so much!" Danielle looked Anthony in his eyes while caressing his cheek. She leaned over and kissed him on the lips.

"I love you too, love. You know you make it sound as if it was easy to forgive you. You make me sound like this perfect person, but I struggled. I just didn't let you see it. When you were in the hospital, I thought my life was over. You do so much for the kids and me. You mean so much to us that I believed what the doctors were saying, but I knew who to call. I may not have had a relationship with God for a while, but I knew who did. My mom. Once she got to that hospital and prayed over you and laid hands on you, I knew it was going to be alright. I had a long talk with God, and I begged him not to take you. I didn't care about this Mike dude. I didn't care about the circumstances that landed you there. I just wanted you to be okay. He brought you out of that coma and restored you to the point where the doctors are still astonished. So yes, they may still be saying that won't have full use of this and that, but they don't know the

God we serve. I've seen miracles and blessings happen every day. I know this will be one of them."

Danita went over to Danielle and Anthony and hugged them tightly. Everyone in the room was crying by now. She told them how much she loved them and how glad she was that Anthony found his way back to the Lord. Her prayers had been answered; she shouted.

"Well, since everyone is already crying, I may as well go ahead and tell what's going on with me." Marie started dabbing the tears away with a tissue. You guys already know it's been almost a year since Marc died and it was hard to cope. It was even harder when I found out that he was basically leading a double life. Since he was an over the road truck driver, he was out of town a lot, which made it easy to create this alternate reality. Marc married another woman and adopted her son." Marie paused because even though she's been dealing with this for almost a month now, it still sounded crazy coming out of her mouth. "I loved Marc and trusted him. I don't know how he could have done this to me, to the boys." Her voice trailed off.

Danita sat next to Marie and consoled her daughter. No one knew what to say except I'm sorry. What can you say to that? What do you do? Everyone else got up and wrapped their arms around Marie as much as they could.

"So, you ask what I'm thankful for? I'm thankful for the truth. I'm not sure that it set me free, but I'm glad I'm not in the dark anymore."

"That's great baby," Danita said, wiping her daughter's tears away. "Chris, it's your turn."

"Okay, I'm thankful for my family. I have a beautiful, wonderful wife. I have good kids that do well in school. I love what I do and the flexibility my career offers."

Chris hesitated as if he was contemplating if he wanted to continue.

"But what you all don't know is that ever since dad died, I've started to drink more often. I used to only have one drink after work once a week. Now it's at the point where I'm drinking several drinks every day. I don't think I'm an alcoholic, but I have started going to AA because I don't want it to get worse." Chris looked away feeling ashamed.

Juanita kissed Chris on the cheek, "I'm very proud of my husband, and I love the fact that he loves us enough to get help. It takes a big person to admit that there is something wrong. I love you, babe."

Chris returned the kiss this time on the lips. "Mom, I believe it's your turn now."

All the gifts were wrapped.

Danita stood, started picking up the presents, and placing them under the tree.

"We all have trials and tribulations, and each one of you have shown that you can overcome them. I'm thankful we're still here." Her eyes started to well up.

"I'm so thankful for my family, my babies, and my grandbabies. God has provided for us for so many years. I just thank Him for giving me all those years with the love of my life, which gave me you all. I love Christmas. I love when we can all gather together and spend this time together. I enjoy you all so much. I love you."

Everyone was in tears by now, but they all got up and rushed Danita with a bear hug. It was nice.

15.

JEREMY

Danita awoke at 7 a.m. She was surprised as to how well she slept the night before, especially after that whole Jeremy incident. She shook her head, still thinking about how he just kept showing up. She would research thoroughly on getting a gate at the entrance on Monday where only her family would have the code. She scurried around her room, trying to be as quiet as possible as she did not want to wake up anyone just yet. Danita took a shower and put on the jogging suit her grandkids bought her last Christmas. She normally would not wear clothes like this but found that it was very comfortable. All the grandkids put their money together to buy her a pink velour jumpsuit, and the jacket had a hoodie. It accentuated her curves. Curves she was not used to showing, but since it was just around the house, she felt it would be okay. Danita headed downstairs and started to cook breakfast. She made pancakes, French toast, scrambled eggs, turkey bacon, turkey sausage, cheese grits, and started on the coffee. Danita normally freshly squeezes the oranges for the orange juice but went ahead and picked some up from the store when she went shopping. The adults started to peel themselves out of bed and headed downstairs. They could not resist the smell of that coffee. The children were already at the door, waiting for their parents to come out.

The children ran down the stairs, screaming and yelling, "Merry Christmas, Nana!"

"Merry Christmas my babies," Danita said as she hugged and kissed each one of her grandkids. "I know you are anxious for those presents, but you know the drill."

The kids let out a sigh in unison, loud enough for Danita to hear it but not with enough attitudes to get sent upstairs and start over. The children headed to the small table to get prepared for breakfast.

"Good Morning; Merry Christmas!" All the adults said in unison.

"Merry Christmas!" Danita hugged and kissed every one of her children and daughters-in-law. They headed to the table to eat.

Danita pulled out her bible and turned to Matthew 1:18-25. She went to the head of the table, said grace over the food and started to read the bible verses while everyone ate. After the reading of the verses, Danita sat down to eat.

It never ceased to amaze her how she could cook all this food, and there was never much for leftovers. It made her smile. She was just thankful that she could afford to feed her family this way. Not to mention the kids and grandkids will have a pretty nice time with their presents this year.

Once all the food was pretty much devoured the grandkids pitched in to do the dishes. The adults put up any leftovers that remained then they let the children tear into the presents. The living room was so loud with the kids' laughter and screaming that she barely heard the doorbell. She headed to the door, but Germaine stopped her. "I got it, ma. You just sit back and relax." He said, kissing her on the forehead. Danita went and sat back down on the couch.

Germaine answered the door, "Can I help you?"

Jeremy was floored. He could not believe the resemblance. He knew this was his son as he looked just like his father when he was young but with little more color. "Um yes, my name is Jeremy. I'm a friend of your mom's. I just wanted to stop by and tell her Merry Christmas."

"Oh, you couldn't call her on the phone and tell her Merry Christmas? How do you know my mom?"

"Um no, I could not call her; I'm a long- time friend." Jeremy tried not to let on how nervous he was.

"Come in. I'll let her know you're here." Germaine motioned for Jeremy to come in but stay in the foyer.

"If you don't mind me asking, are you her son?"

"Yeah. My name is Germaine. Sorry not sure where my manners are." He reached out to shake Jeremy's hand.

"Cool. Nice to meet you." Jeremy smiled.

Germaine headed to the living room and whispered in Danita's ear, "There's someone here to see you."

Danita looked at her son, perplexed. "Really? Who would be visiting today and didn't call me ahead of time?" She continued asking questions as she got up off the couch.

"I asked him the same thing. He said he couldn't call." Germaine said following his mom to the foyer.

She stopped before getting to the foyer and turned around to face Germaine. "Did you say he?"

"Yes, he said his name is Jeremy." Germaine started to continue to walk to the foyer, and Danita stopped him.

"Jeremy? Is he Caucasian and kind of tall?" Danita said, hoping he did not come back.

"Yeah, Mom. He's about my height. Why? What's wrong?" Germaine started to get suspicious. His mom never asks these many questions when guests come.

"Nothing, um, I will go see him. You don't need to come." Danita said motioning for Germaine to go back to the living room.

"Yes, I do. I don't know this dude. I'm not leaving you alone with him." Germaine said in protection mode.

"Sweetie, I'll be fine. I know Jeremy. I'll be fine. Just get back to your family."

"Okay, mom. Are you sure?" He was hesitant but knew he couldn't keep going back and forth with his mom. He will always lose that battle.

"Yes, I'm sure." Danita kissed him on the cheek. "I'll be in there soon."

"Okay if you say so." Germaine looked confused but headed into the living room.

Danita had to keep her composure. He was trippin' to keep coming back like this. She walked up to Jeremy, grabbed him by the arm, and pulled him outside on the porch.

"You have a beautiful home from what I could see. It's just as beautiful inside as it is outside." Jeremy was trying to play peacemaker.

"What do you want, Jeremy?" Danita asked through gritted teeth.

"I know you asked me to stay away, but it is Christmas, and I'm lonely. I used to be able to spend this time with my family, but I don't have anyone left except you and Germaine." Jeremy's eyes started to water.

Danita was not letting his watery eyes change her mind. "Jeremy, I'm sorry you don't have anyone to spend Christmas with, but we are not your family.

Germaine is not your family and I sure as... I'm not your family either." Danita said, still trying her best to maintain her composure and anger.

"Nita. He looks just like my dad. I know you had to have noticed that. I could not believe the resemblance." Jeremy said, smiling. "I wanted to tell him so badly, but I didn't want you upset with me. I really hoped that we could start over." He said, reaching for her hand.

Danita jerked it away. "Look here, Jeremy. I'm trying my best not to go off on you. I suggest that you get off my property right now before I call the police." Danita had her finger in his face.

Jeremy looked Danita in her eyes, "I'm so sorry I hurt you. I wish I could take it back. How long are you going to wait before you tell Germaine about me? He needs to know. I'm going to be honest with you. I keep coming back because it's the only way I can see you and hopefully see him. And it worked! You have not changed a bit. You are still as beautiful as you were then but with more curves. I still have feelings for you. I wish you could believe me when I tell you that I am sorry from the bottom of my heart." Jeremy's tears had fallen by this time.

Danita was just about to go in on Jeremy when the front door swung open. Germaine came out onto the porch. "Mom, do you have something you need to tell me?" He didn't give Jeremy eye contact but was in front of his mom at this point. No smile, no smirk, just straight face.

Danita stumbled back, "Were you listening to our conversation?"

"Mom, do you have something you want to tell me?" Germaine asked again, his voice sterner this time.

"Boy, don't take that tone with me." Danita stumbled back again, but this time it was because she felt lightheaded.

"Danita, go ahead and tell him," Jeremy said, peeking around Germaine.

"You don't talk." Germaine turned around to face Jeremy quick enough to say that and turned right back to his mom.

"I don't think this is the time to discuss this." Danita started to walk towards the front door.

"Funny. That's the same thing you said the other day. And he looks like the same cat I saw leaving your driveway yesterday." Germaine turned to Jeremy, "were you here yesterday?"

Danita glared at Jeremy and shook her head for him not to answer Germaine's questions.

Jeremy looked at Danita and answered, "Yes, I was here yesterday."

Germaine turned back to Danita, "Mom, I need to know what is going on? Who is this dude? Are you dating again, and you didn't want to tell us? What is going on?" His voice got deeper and sterner.

Tears started to roll down Danita's face. "I didn't want you to find out this way, Maine. I didn't." She walked over to the porch swing and plopped down. "I didn't want you to find out at all, let alone like this."

Germaine walked over to the swing and sat down next to his mother. "Find out what, Ma?"

"That I'm your father." Jeremy chimed in.

Germaine jumped up, punched Jeremy in the mouth, and busted his lip. "What you say? Say it again! I have a father."

Danita jumped up to pull Germaine back, "Maine stop! He's right. He's your biological father. He's not your father. You had a father, and he died. This man is your biological father." Danita plopped back down again on the swing as if saying it aloud exhausted her.

Germaine stared at his mom in disbelief. "How could that be? That doesn't make sense. Dad has always been here. I don't understand. Help me to understand!" Germaine's voice was stern and deep again.

"Since you blurted it out, you want to tell him the whole story? Or, are you going to make me do the honors?" Danita asked Jeremy feeling aggrieved that it was going down this way.

"Um well. I was, I mean. Your mom and I dated in high school. We were really in love. We moved in together after we graduated. We both had great jobs. Well, um, you see." Jeremy took a deep breath and sighed as if it would make what he was about to say better. "One night I went out with my friends and got drunk. They started talking trash, and I believed what they said. I came home and..." Jeremy stopped not wanting to say the terrible thing he had done.

"You came home and?" Germaine was anxious for him to complete this story so it could make sense.

"I forced myself onto your mom. I went to jail for rape and assault and battery. I found out about you when I was in jail. I wrote to your mom several times, but my letters were returned. When I got out, I met a woman, got married, and we had a child. They were killed in a car accident. I came looking for you and Nita. I'm so sorry I caused her so much pain. I just wanted to get to know you." Jeremy said, trying to fight back the tears but was unsuccessful.

Germaine shook his head in disbelief, "Mom is this true?" He was crying. "Mom is this true?" He had dropped to his knees to kneel in front of her.

"Yes, son, it's true. He left out all the gory details but in a nutshell that's what happened. I became pregnant from him forcing himself on me, but I don't believe in abortion, so I kept you and raised you, and loved you every day. I didn't feel like you needed to know about him, so I never said anything." Tears steadily streamed down her face. "I met your father when you were two-years-old and were together until he died."

To be continued…

ABOUT THE AUTHOR

A'Driana was born and raised in Atlanta, Georgia. She's a wife of 21 years with two sons. Her curiosity with writing began when she was young being an avid reader. It peaked in high school with English and Literature being her favorite subjects. After having her oldest son, her love and passion for writing increased and 18 years later, Tryals & Trybulations is complete.

She continues to work as a Technical Chat Advisor at Kelly Connect and before that, she was a Resolution Expeditor at The Home Depot for close to 9 years.

What's next? A'Driana is currently working on the follow up to Tryals & Trybulations. She's started several other writing projects as well. And, looking to work with as many up and coming writers with the ends and outs of this process as she can.

www.ingramcontent.com/pod-product-compliance
Lightning Source LLC
Chambersburg PA
CBHW051837090426
42736CB00011B/1847